FULLY DEVOTED

FOLLOWING JESUS ONE STEP AT A TIME

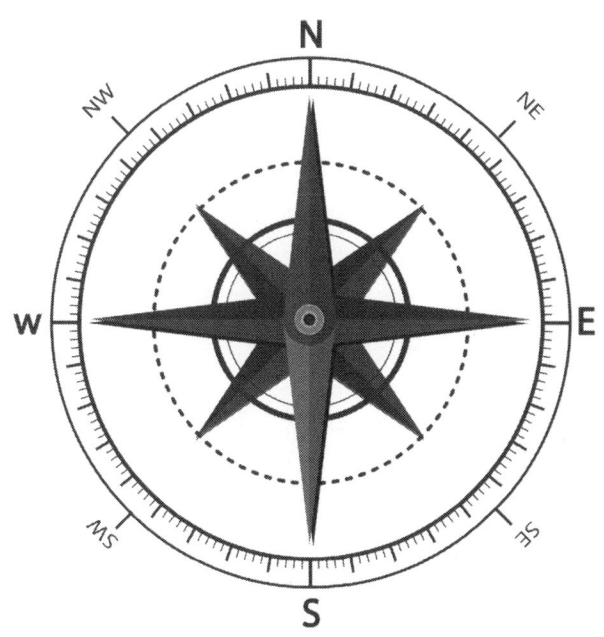

ANTHONY D. DALEY

*

May we exist to create fully devoted

followers of Jesus Christ.

ACKNOWLEDGMENTS

No one has impacted my life more than my wife, Julia. Together, we have taken each step on this journey. I am eternally grateful for her and the family she has given me—infinity times infinity!

—

I want to thank Kyle Lawley, who has been an integral part of this journey, going chapter by chapter with me and ensuring that we stayed on target. Big Love!

—

I want to thank Susan Willets for her insights and help in preparing the final draft. God makes us all better together!

—

I want to thank Joseph Mendes, who has ridden this roller coaster with me and always makes me look much better than I am. He's a rockstar in my life!

TABLE OF CONTENTS

INTRODUCTION

I encounter many people who love the idea of being a Christian. The teachings and character of Jesus are inspirational. After all, how could you not like Jesus? Look at all the awesome things He did to help people. The pinnacle being that He died for us. Who wouldn't love someone who laid down his or her life for you?

The benefits of what they perceive Christianity to be are desirable. Forgiveness, eternal life in heaven, happiness, and peace are all offered to those who believe. The decision is a no-brainer, especially considering that most people who come to Jesus find Him while living in a difficult place.

Many scenes play out like this. You get up on Sunday morning and go to a church you've heard about, or someone invited you to. You arrive feeling a bit nervous and out of your element of comfort. The worship begins, and you're not sure how you should respond, but your inner voice whispers, "This could be the day." The minister shares a compelling message and promises the new life in Christ will be an incredible journey, free from all the bondage of the past and present trials. Your emotions and hope are raised within you like never before. You want a more meaningful life.

The message ends, and everyone is asked to "bow your heads with no one looking around." The minister is creating a private moment for those in a decision-making place. It is an attempt to shield you from any reluctance that might arise from being embarrassed or singled out. Then the question comes, "While every head is bowed and no one is looking around, if you are here today and would like to receive Jesus as your Lord and Savior, please raise your hand." You slowly raise your hand; the preacher acknowledges, "I see your hand." After a few more exhortations by the minister, "Anyone else?" You then are asked to repeat a prayer to receive Christ as your Lord and Savior.

For the church community it's called "the sinners prayer." It goes something like this. "Dear heavenly Father, I believe Jesus is your Son. I believe He died on the cross for my sins. I believe He was resurrected from the dead after three days to give me eternal life. I ask you to come into my heart and forgive me of all my sins. Amen!"

The preacher continues, "Would everyone clap your hands and celebrate with those who made Jesus the Lord of their life today." The congregation claps their hands with a few shouts of celebration.

The preacher concludes, "God bless everyone, we'll see you next week." That's it! You're a Christian.

For most, the felt expectation is to come back to church next week. Unfortunately, many often don't grow past this point. They leave the church and find life around them has not changed at all. Without understanding where you go from here, you may simply settle back into what has always been familiar.

The truth is, you just took your first step—it's one step! There are many more in front of you as you endeavor to live a life of faith. This book will guide you through the next steps of your journey toward being a fully devoted follower of Jesus.

The importance of the path ahead may differ from the order of steps in which this book is laid out. However, if you are going to live the Christian life to its fullest and experience all of the benefits, you must continue to take the next step.

SECTION ONE

First Steps

Acts 2:37–39 (NKJV) Now when they heard this, they were cut to the heart, and said to Peter and the rest of the apostles, "Men and brethren, what shall we do?" Then Peter said to them, "Repent, and let every one of you be baptized in the name of Jesus Christ for the remission of sins; and you shall receive the gift of the Holy Spirit. For the promise is to you and to your children, and to all who are afar off, as many as the Lord our God will call."

CHAPTER ONE

Salvation

*

"That's one small step for man, one giant leap for mankind."
- Neil Armstrong.

July 20th, 1969, is forever a day enshrined in history. It would be the day Commander Neil Armstrong and Lunar Module Pilot Buzz Aldrin landed the Apollo Lunar Module Eagle on the moon. Exiting the lunar spacecraft, Neil Armstrong would become the first man to step onto the moon's surface. His initial response would become iconic, "That's one small step for man, one giant leap for mankind." That day, anything seemed possible to the watching world. Mesmerized by the images of Earth from the moon, we gained a new perspective of ourselves. It was truly the next step in human history. Over the last 50-plus years, his words continue to speak to the power of a moment defined by one step.

For me, that day reminds me of my beginning. My mother recalls being in labor and delivery while watching that lunar landing on July 20th, 1969. I would be born a few hours later, on July 21st. Over the next 29 years, my steps would be all over the place. My perspective of the world around me was shaped by our poverty, being raised by a single mom, and my neighborhood. The environment in which I was immersed influenced my decision-making and values. However, twenty-nine years later, everything would change with one step.

On July 21, 1998, I found myself drowning in drug addiction. My marriage, after ten years, stood on the edge of collapse. My business was bankrupt, and I was too. I came home at about 3:00 AM. I had spent the previous twelve hours drinking and doing drugs. I went to the bedroom, where my wife was already asleep. Trying to be discreet and avoid any confrontation, I slipped into bed. This would become a defining moment. I was about to take the biggest step of my life. As I lay there on the bed, a deep darkness surrounded me.

In my hopelessness, I asked the Lord to rescue me from the darkness. As if I heard His voice say, "I already have. I've sent Jesus."

Moved with indescribable emotions, I got out of bed, knelt on the floor, and asked Jesus into my life. For many, that may seem like one small step, but it was a giant leap for me. I was lost, and suddenly, I was saved.

OPERATION HOPE

On May 1, 2023, a small Cessna plane traveled across the Amazon Rain Forest. Inside the plane was a mother and her four children, ages 13, 9, and 4, plus an 11-month-old baby and two other adults. The plane's engine started to malfunction, causing it to crash in a dense area of the Amazon. The Colombian military launched Operation Hope to find the aircraft. It would take two weeks for rescue crews to find the downed plane.

Rappelling, down to the forest floor, they found the bodies of three adults, including the mother of the children; however, all four children were missing. A relentless search occurred over the next three weeks to find the kids. On one occasion during the rescue, it was discovered that they were within yards of the children, who were hiding in fear. To calm their fears, the kids' grandmother recorded a message in the Huitoto language that was broadcast into the jungle.

On day 40, they found the children in a patch of rainforest so thick there was no place for the rescue helicopter to land. As the chopper hovered overhead, troops rappelled to the jungle floor and hoisted the children back up to the aircraft. The miracle of the story is that the children, with their infant sibling, survived forty days in this hostile environment (Otis).

The children were hopelessly lost and needed a rescue party. That's how humanity looked for four thousand years after Adam and Eve fell in the Garden of Eden. God responded by sending out the search party.

LOST OR SAVED

In Christianity, people are defined as being in one of two categories. People are either lost or saved. If a person is considered 'lost,' it's as if they have been dropped in the Amazon rainforest without proper clothing, nothing to protect themselves with, or a compass to guide them to safety. Their life is lived under constant threat, buried in hopelessness, and no way to find their way out. If a person is considered 'saved,' they are those who were in the rainforest with all the hopelessness and threats, then someone rappelled down, saved them and brought them out.

Every human being begins this life journey lost. Why are we lost? We are separated from our God and creator due to disobedience by the first human beings, Adam and Eve. It wasn't His intention in the beginning. No!

> Genesis 1:27–28 (NKJV) "So God created man in His own image; in the image of God He created him; male and female He created them. Then God blessed them, and God said to them, "Be fruitful and multiply; fill the earth and subdue it; have dominion over the fish of the sea, over the birds of the air, and over every living thing that moves on the earth."

He created us with the capacity to communicate with Him; we're in His image and likeness. He blessed mankind with the ability to reproduce and populate the world with others who would have a relationship with Him. He gave mankind the power to rule over all creation. No, in the beginning, no one was lost in the Amazon.

God planted a garden and gave man a new home with all the provisions needed. Genesis 2:8–9 (NKJV) "The LORD God planted a garden eastward in Eden, and there He put the man whom He had formed. And out of the ground the LORD God made every tree grow that is pleasant to the sight and good for food…"

It was not work God called mankind to; it was a relationship.

God created the perfect environment and companion for fellowship. He would come to share with Adam and Eve in the garden Genesis 3:8 (NKJV) "And they heard the sound of the LORD God walking in the garden in the cool of the day…"

What an amazing time that must have been. Mankind in the perfect environment speaks to God, the creator of it all. A personal and meaningful relationship between the creator and His creation.

CHOICE IS A GIFT

One of God's greatest gifts to humanity is the power of choice. The ability to reason and choose is unique to human beings alone. Genesis 2:16–17 (NKJV) "And the LORD God commanded the man, saying, "Of every tree of the garden you may freely eat; but of the tree of the knowledge of good and evil you shall not eat, for in the day that you eat of it you shall surely die."

God gave the man a choice. The choice was not between good and evil. The choice was between a relationship with God or a life filled with a fight between good and evil.

Unfortunately, mankind has a manipulative enemy called the devil. He is also referred to as the deceiver, the evil one, and Satan. He disguised himself as a serpent and enticed mankind into making the wrong decision. Genesis 3:1 (NKJV) "Now the serpent was more cunning than any beast of the field which the LORD God had made. And he said to the woman, "Has God indeed said, 'You shall not eat of every tree of the garden'?"

The devil's primary strategy is to create doubt in God. You are heading down the wrong path once you start into the conversation of doubt.

The consequences of the wrong choice were disastrous for mankind. Adam and Eve chose to eat the fruit from the tree God told them to refrain from (Genesis 3:6).

It was at this point that sin entered into the world, and the world as God intended would be lost. Romans 5:12 (NKJV) "Therefore, just as through one man sin entered the world, and death through sin, and thus death spread to all men, because all sinned."

Let me briefly define sin. In the New Testament, which was originally written in the Greek language, sin is defined as "to miss the mark, to be mistaken. To miss or wander from the path of uprightness and honor, to do or go wrong." (Logos Library System).

Let me illustrate: It's like an archer with his bow, arrow, and a target in front of him. When the arrow is released from the bow, the sight has been set on a target. God is the archer with the bow. You and I are the arrows. The target is God's purpose and destination for our lives. God has launched our lives towards the target. When the arrow veers off its path and misses the target, that is called missing the mark. This is what sin is! Missing the mark God has for your life. While He points us toward the target, our choices determine our path. We can choose God's way and hit the target or do it our way and miss the mark: sin.

Adam and Eve missed the mark God had set for them, and now they're on another path. They would be expelled from the Garden of Eden and dropped into the "Amazon jungle" of this world. Genesis 3:23 (NLT) "So the LORD God banished them from the Garden of Eden, and he sent Adam out to cultivate the ground from which he had been made."

SEARCH PARTY OF ONE

For the next four thousand years, man would wander aimlessly in his "Amazon," needing a search party to rescue him. Well, it wasn't a large search party; while many people were pivotal throughout history, it was a one-man search party. His name is Jesus. His assignment was clear:

> Luke 19:10 (NLT) "For the Son of Man came to seek and save those who are lost."

It took the grandmother's voice to bring the children to safety; likewise, Jesus calls out to our souls. Jesus likens us all to sheep and says His sheep know His voice (John 10:40). Over the last two thousand years, Jesus has been rescuing all those who hear and respond to His voice.

Those who put their faith in Him, we call saved! Romans 10:9 (NKJV) "That if you confess with your mouth the Lord Jesus and believe in your heart that God has raised Him from the dead, you will be saved."

When the lost children in the Amazon heard the rescue team, they hid. Adam and Eve did the same thing when God searched for them (Genesis 3:8). They hid in their fear and shame. But our God is determined to find us, and He sent the greatest rescuer of all time, Jesus!

The biggest step you will ever take is calling out to Jesus. He will use every circumstance as an opportunity to rescue you and restore your life as God intended. When you call out to Him, like the soldiers rescuing the children, He will descend into your life, lift you out of sin, and restore your life.

I was saved that night in July, pulled out from my hiding. It was one small step to the world around me but a giant step toward a new beginning for me and my family.

CHAPTER TWO

Born Again

*

"How can an old man go back into his mother's womb and be born again?"
- Nicodemus

I was sitting there on my knees sobbing profusely, in desperate need of change. When the tears dried, I quietly crawled back into the bed on that pivotal night in July 1998. I fell fast asleep. When I woke in the morning, something was different. I felt different. It wasn't because my situation had drastically changed. I was still sitting in the aftermath of bankruptcy. I woke up to a wife who was still frustrated with our marriage. I could still hear the voice of my addiction insisting on controlling me. But the hopelessness was gone, and I felt a new strength. Something happened on the floor that night. A new man had awakened the following day.

Isn't it funny that a dirty man can feel clean even when wearing the same clothes? How can a broken man feel healed when still standing in the brokenness? How does a man who felt so much shame suddenly feel accepted? How can a man chained by addiction suddenly feel free?

What happened to me when I called out to Jesus? I was saved, but it was more than that. I was born again.

"Born again" is a phrase Jesus uses to describe the new state of being that comes from experiencing salvation.

> John 3:3 (NLT) Jesus replied, "I tell you the truth, unless you are born again, you cannot see the Kingdom of God."

Being born again is the next step towards discovering God's desired relationship with you.

This very educated leader in Israel, Nicodemus, struggled to understand this unique experience as Jesus shared. He tried to imagine it as a natural experience. "How can an old man get back into his mother's womb?" he asked. (John 3:4 (NLT)) Obviously, Jesus wasn't speaking about a natural rebirth but a spiritual one. Being born again happens on the inside. Jesus said it is mysterious, like the wind, which you can feel but can't see. John 3:8 (NLT) "The wind blows wherever it wants. Just as you can hear the wind but can't tell where it comes from or where it is going, so you can't explain how people are born of the Spirit." On the outside, everything looks the same, but new life is pounding on the inside. You can't explain it! You didn't see it coming, but like the wind, you sure felt it.

HEREDITARY SIN

When God told Adam and Eve that death would be the consequence of their sin, He was very serious. Genesis 2:17 (NLT) "… If you eat its fruit, you are sure to die." So, the result of sin, missing the mark, was death. Adam and Eve would die sometime after eating from the Tree of the Knowledge of Good and Evil. When they sinned, death was the penalty. When we sin, the penalty is still enforced - Romans 6:23 (NLT) "For the wages of sin is death…" Unless the wage is paid, of course.

Because Adam is the father of humanity, we've all inherited his nature. He was a sinner, and we have all inherited a sinful nature. (Romans 5:12)

I was raised by a single mom. My father wasn't around much when I was growing up, and even into my teenage years, I didn't see him much. So, his influence on my attitude, outlook, and mannerisms was minimal. You might say he was just the sperm donor. However, when you see my dad and I, our physical similarities tell you we are father and son: same hair color, same build, same eye color.

Thankfully, for the last twenty-five years, I have had the opportunity to live close to my father. Being around him has allowed me a front-row seat to observe his idiosyncrasies; I've been quite astonished. There are so many similarities between him and me. In the things he does, how he does them, his body language, and even how he processes situations. I didn't get them by observation or experience; I inherited them by blood.

THE POWER OF THE BLOOD

Life of the flesh is the blood (Leviticus 17:14). It is the blood that brings life to the flesh. The body has numerous types of tissue: muscle, nerves, fat, glands, bone, connective tissue, etc. They have one thing in common: they are fixed cells. The blood is fluid and mobile and not limited to one part of the body. Your body has about ten pints of blood, which the heart pumps through the body every twenty-three seconds. This blood supplies fuel and cleanses and protects every cell in the body. There is power in the blood!

Red blood cells, called erythrocytes, are a large concentration of cells (about 5 mil per cubic mm) that pass through the lungs, pick up oxygen, and carry it throughout the body. The fuel is discharged to the cells. Then, after nourishing the cells, it carries off the waste products, or "ashes" of cell activity (carbon dioxide and tissue metabolism waste), and discards it through the liver, kidneys, skin, bowels, and lungs.

If the blood fails to reach a cell, it dies. Death comes when the blood ceases to circulate. A man doesn't die because he's shot with a gun. He dies because the shot lets the blood out. He bleeds out. Life is in the blood!

White blood cells, called leukocytes, are larger than red blood cells and fewer in number. Whereas the red cells are about 5 million in a cubic centimeter, the white cells are about 5-7 thousand. They are called the standing army of the bloodstream. When the body gets attacked with a virus, infection, stress, or trauma, the news is flashed to the manufacturer of white blood cells, and immediately, the increased number of cells rush to the point of attack.

The white blood cells have a strange power to kill germs and put the body in fight mode. For example, when you get cut, swelling will start around a wound. This is where the conscript of soldiers circle the point of attack. Millions of the soldiers are killed in the attack along with partly digested germs that form a 'pus.' The pus is ultimately forced out of the body. This is followed by more white cells that come and rebuild the tissue, and you heal. This is why the doctor pricks your finger for a blood test. If your white blood cell count is up, you have an infection. There is healing in the blood! (Cleveland Clinic).

The Bible is a book about blood sacrifice and blood covenants. When Adam and Eve sinned in the garden in Genesis chapter 3, God came down and sacrificed an animal to provide a covering for Adam and Eve. In Genesis chapter 9, God and Noah make a covenant with animal sacrifice. The pattern continues in Genesis chapter 15 in the covenantal agreement with God and Abraham. The entire Jewish nation was freed from slavery in Egypt by the blood of a lamb in Exodus chapter 12. The sacrifices and covenant culminate in the sacrifice of Jesus, giving us a New Testament covenant, as He describes in Matthew 26.

As Christians, we sing songs about the blood:

"Are you washed in the blood of the lamb? Are your garments spotless? Are they white as snow? Are you washed in the blood of the lamb?" (Hoffman).

"There is power, power, wonder-working power in the blood of the lamb" (Lewis Edgar Jones).

Like a newborn baby, your new life is filled with learning. Most importantly, learning to talk. As followers of Jesus, we have language describing what is happening. One such expression to describe being born again is 'washed in the blood.' Now, for most people, that sounds a bit crazy. But spiritually, that is precisely what happens when you are born again. Our entire faith rests upon being washed in blood - Revelation 1:5 (NKJV) "...To Him who loved us and washed us from our sins in His own blood."

That blood flows into your spirit and brings life to your spirit man, like the red blood cells, while simultaneously carrying away the sin contaminating your life. That blood forms an army, just like the white blood cells, fighting off every attack the enemy tries to infect your life with. There is power in the blood.

THE CROSS

"Houston, we've had a problem!" It was April 13, 1970, when the now famous words were spoken from Apollo 13. Apollo 13 had just experienced an explosion, and astronaut Jim Lovell called mission control in Houston to report the problem. The crew now faces many scenarios, one of which is being lost in the darkness of the universe. The Apollo 13 crew and NASA had to overcome several serious obstacles to return home. The country was captivated by the plight of the astronauts, and on April 18, the crew splashed down safely in the ocean ("Houston, We've Had a Problem, Spoken from Space").

Humanity, we have a problem! Sin gave humanity a blood disease (Romans 5:12). Like Apollo 13, there were some obstacles to overcome to cancel the inevitability of death that humanity faced. Without a solution, we would all be lost in the abyss of eternal darkness. So our God provided a way for us all to find our way back home, the blood of Jesus.

> Romans 5:17 (NLT) "For the sin of this one man, Adam, caused death to rule over many. But even greater is God's wonderful grace and his gift of righteousness, for all who receive it will live in triumph over sin and death through this one man, Jesus Christ."

When it comes to Jesus, He wasn't a son of Adam. No, He is the Son of

God. Born in the womb of a virgin named Mary (Luke 1:27). She conceived through the Holy Spirit (Luke 1:35). The blood of humanity was contaminated and brought death to the body. So, God sent a new bloodline. His blood is precious and to be highly valued. 1 Peter 1:19 (NLT) "It was the precious blood of Christ, the sinless, spotless Lamb of God."

Jesus' blood had no sin contaminants and would cleanse the body from the sinful diseases that brought death. Joel 3:21 (KJV) "For I will cleanse their blood that I have not cleansed: For the LORD dwelleth in Zion." His blood would flow through our life, bringing health and wholeness while removing the toxin of sin's nature.

His blood would also protect the body as the white blood cells do. Fighting against any attempt of infiltration by this world we live in and causing death to be expelled. 1 Corinthians 15:57 (NLT) "But thank God! He gives us victory over sin and death through our Lord Jesus Christ."

Praise God for the blood of Jesus!

The cross, a tool the Romans used for torture and death, is the instrument in which the blood would be taken.

> Colossians 1:20 (NLT) "and through him God reconciled everything to himself. He made peace with everything in heaven and on earth by means of Christ's blood on the cross."

The Romans used the cross as a tool for torture.

Public crucifixions were meant to strike fear in the hearts of the onlookers and to inflict excruciating pain on those being nailed to the trees. But God used what the enemy meant for evil for good. The cross was a gruesome, painful way for Jesus to die, and our hearts mourn over His suffering. However, we find acceptance and love when we look to the cross. Love was the reason God sent His Son to the cross (John 3:16).

Death was the cost of sin, so Jesus paid the price for all humanity. 1

Corinthians 15:3 (NLT) "…Christ died for our sins." He died for us all. On that glorious day, I received a spiritual blood transfusion, and I was free and forgiven. Hebrews 9:22 (NLT) "…For without the shedding of blood, there is no forgiveness." All my sins washed away!

Praise God for the blood of Jesus!

MORE THAN A FEELING

Here is how it works: When you confess with your mouth and believe in your heart in Jesus's death, burial, and resurrection, you invite the Holy Spirit into your life. Romans 10:9–10 (NKJV) "That if you confess with your mouth the Lord Jesus and believe in your heart that God has raised Him from the dead, you will be saved. For with the heart one believes unto righteousness, and with the mouth confession is made unto salvation."

The Holy Spirit is God's breath and life. When He comes, He brings grace and forgiveness to your life. Romans 5:5 (NKJV) "…because the love of God has been poured out in our hearts by the Holy Spirit who was given to us."

You are now a Christian!

The disciples were not saved because they walked with Jesus while He was alive. They weren't saved because they thought He was God's son due to the miracles they witnessed. They, like you and I, must believe in the resurrection. When Jesus appears to them after the resurrection, this happens.

> John 20:22 (NKJV) "And when He had said this, He breathed on them, and said to them, "Receive the Holy Spirit. When they witnessed His resurrection, the Holy Spirit came."

When you call out to Jesus, the Holy Spirit comes into your life and validates the love and forgiveness that has taken place. Romans 8:16 (NKJV) "The Spirit Himself bears witness with our spirit that we are children of God."

The Holy Spirit causes me to feel and sense emotionally and spiritually that I am born again. Remember Nicodemus in John 3:8? You can feel the wind; you can't see it. The Holy Spirit causes you to feel born again, loved, and accepted by God. He confirms that you have been forgiven of all your sins; the slate was wiped clean, and you are given a new beginning. Yes, it's a bit mysterious, as Jesus indicated, but real nonetheless.

Those born again have been adopted into God's family. A divine exchange has occurred, and we are now reunited with God. You gave Him your sin, and He placed you back in right standing, like Adam in the garden before sin.

> 2 Corinthians 5:21 (NKJV) "For He made Him who knew no sin to be sin for us, that we might become the righteousness of God in Him."

KEEP REMEMBERING

The cross was the tool used, but the body and blood of Jesus are the gift given to us all. Before Jesus' death, He taught the disciples about communion. Communion is when we pause and reflect on what Jesus has done for our lives. You will take juice, representing His blood, and a piece of bread, representing His body, and eat them while remembering that He gave His body and blood for your life. Jesus told His disciples to remember Him every time they took communion.

> Matthew 26:26–28 (NKJV) "And as they were eating, Jesus took bread, blessed and broke it, and gave it to the disciples and said, "Take, eat; this is My body." Then He took the cup, and gave thanks, and gave it to them, saying, "Drink from it, all of you. For this is My blood of the new covenant, which is shed for many for the remission of sins."

When we share the sacraments of communion, we are reminded each time that His blood has saved us, forgiven us, and given us eternal life.

When life hits you hard and doubt rises in your heart, always remember: you are an overcomer by His blood and your faith in Him. Revelation 12:11 (NKJV) "And they overcame him by the blood of the Lamb and by the word of their testimony, and they did not love their lives to the death."

The step to being born again has taken place inside of you. It is a private and personal experience that launches you into a brand-new way of living. The next step is letting the world know.

CHAPTER THREE

Water Baptism

*

"Baptism is an outward expression of an inward faith."
- Watchman Nee

As a kid growing up around the church, I was part of many water baptisms. In our church, it wasn't uncommon for kids to take advantage of the moment when the church went to the creek to baptize new believers and get baptized again. Maybe it was just an excuse to get in the water, but I was familiar with the experience. I'm uncertain about the number of times that I've been baptized, but I remember the one that meant something.

Shortly after I was saved, my job sent me to North Carolina. My wife and family were very concerned if I would continue to live for Jesus. While there, I had a strong sense that I needed to repeat things I did as a kid when I started following Jesus. Doing your first works over was what Jesus asked the Church of Ephesus to do in Revelation 2. They had drifted away, and He was calling them to return. Well, I had drifted away many times, but now I was back and more determined than ever to be a fully devoted follower of Jesus.

I returned from North Carolina for the weekend and went to church that Sunday morning. It was a cold February afternoon in Tennessee. I had been saved for about eight months, and I wanted to take the next step; this time, I meant it. I asked a friend to take me to the creek and baptize me. It was cold, but I was eager to publicly demonstrate my commitment to everyone that I follow Jesus.

I've heard many discussions throughout the years about water baptism. Is it even essential to be water-baptized? After all, the thief on the cross wasn't baptized (Luke 23:43). Some say, "I was baptized when I was a kid", or "I was sprinkled when I was an infant, and there's no need to do it again." For me, baptism is not about when it was done or even how often it was done. It's about why it is done.

A BRIEF HISTORY

When we begin reading our Bibles in the first book, Genesis 1:2, we discover that the earth is completely submerged in water. It was from this position that God would call life forth. Hidden beneath the surface was the land, trees, fruit, and the very dirt from which man would be made. Over six days, God would call forth life out of those waters.

As mankind became corrupt after the fall of Adam and Eve, God chose a righteous man named Noah to build a boat. God was about to judge humanity because of sin, and He was going to use water to do it. We would see the earth submerged in water, sinful humanity buried in the depths below, and the righteous Noah rising to the surface in his ark of safety. The apostle Peter would liken the flood to water baptism.

> 1 Peter 3:20–21 (NLT) "Those who disobeyed God long ago when God waited patiently while Noah was building his boat. Only eight people were saved from drowning in that terrible flood. And that water is a picture of baptism, which now saves you, not by removing dirt from your body, but as a response to God from a clean conscience. It is effective because of the resurrection of Jesus Christ."

The Pharaoh of Egypt, in the book of Exodus, chapter 2, had issued the order to kill all the male children in Egypt. Moses was placed in an ark and sent down the river. Pharaoh's daughter would find him and pull him from the water, essentially saving his life. The name Moses means to be drawn out, commemorating how he was drawn from the water.

When the nation of Israel was rescued from slavery and sent forth from Egypt, they would find themselves facing the Red Sea. A wind would blow through the entire night, parting the waters of the Red Sea, and the entire nation would pass through the Red Sea on dry ground. The apostle Paul likens this moment to the baptism of the entire nation of Israel after they had experienced the salvation made possible by the lamb's blood at Passover (Exodus 12).

> 1 Corinthians 10:2 (NLT) "In the cloud and in the sea, all of them were baptized as followers of Moses."

The New Testament opens with an introduction to John the Baptist, who calls the nation of Israel into repentance. John's baptism provides the people with a public platform to demonstrate their repentance.

Jesus is introduced to us at the launch of His public ministry in Matthew chapter 3, being baptized by John in the Jordan River. This was His first public display, which became a catalyst and an example of the power of water baptism.

When we are born again, it is a private internal work that happens to our spirit. The next step is to let the world know what you have experienced. Water baptism is the first way we begin to share our faith. It has three powerful meanings:

1. Public Confession
2. Identity
3. Commissioning

PUBLIC CONFESSION

Getting water baptized is not meant to be a private matter. Historically, it has been performed in the audience of the church community. The baptism ceremony is an open statement to the world that I now follow Jesus. When Jesus's ministry begins, He goes down to the Jordan River to see John the Baptist, who is baptizing. When John sees him coming, he initially refuses to baptize Jesus. But Jesus pushes back and tells

John we must do things correctly. We must do it God's way (Matthew 3:15).

When leading people to the "prayer of salvation" we use Romans 10:9 (KJV) "That if thou shalt confess with thy mouth the Lord Jesus, and shalt believe in thine heart that God hath raised him from the dead, thou shalt be saved."

Rightly so, it tells us how we are saved. But two things are of note in the text. One is believing in your heart. This is the place where our born-again experience happens. The grace of God saves us through faith.

Second is confessing with your mouth. During the baptismal ceremony, you will be asked if you believe that Jesus died on the cross and rose from the dead for your life. With your answer, you have informed everybody that you believe in the death, burial, and resurrection of Jesus.

> Colossians 2:12 (NLT) "For you were buried with Christ when you were baptized. And with him you were raised to new life because you trusted the mighty power of God, who raised Christ from the dead."

The ceremony itself is a re-enactment. You are confessing by going down into the water that you are crucified with Christ, and when you come out of the water, you are declaring you are being raised to a new life. Romans 6:3–4 (NLT) "Or have you forgotten that when we were joined with Christ Jesus in baptism, we joined him in his death? For we died and were buried with Christ by baptism. And just as Christ was raised from the dead by the glorious power of the Father, now we also may live new lives."

With your confession of faith, you proclaim you are a new person living on a new journey.

IDENTITY

Our name is how we are identified. When your name is mentioned, it also comes with a definition. The definition is based on the lifestyle we're living.

To be called a Christian is an honorable thing. The word was first used in Acts 11:26 (NLT) "….It was at Antioch that the believers were first called Christians." The Greek word is Christianos, which means 'a follower of Christ' (Logos Library System). The people of Antioch followed the teaching of Jesus to such an extent that their neighbors identified them as "belonging to Christ."

Baptism is a place where identity is given. In historical times, when a person was baptized, they were immersed in someone's identity. For example, those who followed Moses to the Red Sea were said to be baptized as followers of Moses. 1 Corinthians 10:2 (NLT) "In the cloud and in the sea, all of them were baptized as followers of Moses."

The apostle Paul, in Acts 19, encounters a group of disciples who identify with the baptism of John the Baptist. Acts 19:3 (NLT) "Then what baptism did you experience?" he asked. And they replied, "The baptism of John."

When Jesus was baptized, God released His identity.

> Matthew 3:17 (NLT) "And a voice from heaven said, "This is my dearly loved Son, who brings me great joy."

Coming out of the water, God identified Jesus publicly as His Son.

Jesus told the disciples to baptize people in His name. Matthew 28:19 (NLT) "Therefore, go and make disciples of all the nations, baptizing them in the name of the Father and the Son and the Holy Spirit."

In most Protestant churches, when you are baptized, the person responsible for baptizing will say, "I baptize you in the name of the Father and of the Son and the Holy Spirit." There are some church denominations that will say, "I baptize you in the name of Jesus." They get this language from other passages, such as Acts 19:5 (NLT) "As soon as they heard this, they were baptized in the name of the Lord Jesus."

While this can become a debate among some Christians, for me, it is not something worth debating. If someone who baptizes you says, "In the name of the Father, Son, and Holy Spirit" or "In the name of Jesus," it's the same. Because the Father, Son, and Holy Spirit are One!

Honestly, what is said when you're being baptized is important, but not as important as what you believe and how you live afterward. I mean, say you get baptized, and the right things are said, but when you come out of the water, you still live like the old you. That's a problem. Remember that being called a Christian means that you live like Christ.

When you're baptized, your identity is now in Jesus.

COMMISSIONING

In the temple of the Old Testament, there was a bronze laver filled with water. The priests in charge of the House of God used the laver. These priests who were responsible for bridging the gap between God and the Jewish people were called Levites. Levites were one of the twelve sons of Jacob in the Old Testament. These twelve great-grandsons of Abraham became the nation of Israel. The Levites were chosen to be the priests who oversaw the Temple of God. Their priestly responsibilities began at thirty years of age. Numbers 4:47 (NLT) "All the men between thirty and fifty years of age who were eligible for service in the Tabernacle and for its transportation."

At the age of 30, a Levite would come to the bronze laver, remove his clothing, wash in the water, and then put on a white robe. This was called the commissioning ceremony for the priesthood. Leviticus 16:4 (NLT) "He must put on his linen tunic and the linen undergarments worn next to his body. He must tie the linen sash around his waist and put the linen turban on his head. These are sacred garments, so he must bathe himself in water before he puts them on."

This is why Jesus would be baptized at 30 years of age. His ministry could not begin at 29 years old; He had to wait until 30 years of age to do it God's way. Luke 3:23 (KJV) "And Jesus himself began to be about thirty years of age, being (as was supposed) the son of Joseph, which was the son of Heli."

Remember His words to John in Matthew 3:15? We must do it God's way! For the priests of the Old Testament, it was their day of release. From that day forward, they were commissioned into the ministry of the Lord. For Jesus, the day of His baptism was His commissioning and His release to the work God called. He was clothed that day as well. Not with a new robe but with the Holy Spirit, who would empower His ministry. Matthew 3:16 (NLT) "After his baptism, as Jesus came up out of the water, the heavens were opened and he saw the Spirit of God descending like a dove and settling on him."

Baptism is about making my public confession and establishing my identity as a Christian, but equally as important, it is the day we are commissioned to take the good news about Jesus to all the world. We come to the water with our old clothes on, and spiritually, we put on a new linen robe, like the priest of old. Our robe is spiritual, we are now in the right standing with God. Revelation 19:8 (NKJV) "And to her it was granted to be arrayed in fine linen, clean and bright, for the fine linen is the righteous acts of the saints."

However, it's not the Old Testament Priest we follow. No, we are putting on the ministry robe of Jesus.

> Galatians 3:27 (NLT) "And all who have been united with Christ in baptism have put on Christ, like putting on new clothes."

In this new attire and commissioning, we now assume the responsibility to share Jesus with the world. Revelation 1:6 (NLT) "He has made us a Kingdom of priests for God his Father. All glory and power to him forever and ever! Amen."

NEW WAY

I had been baptized many times before that cold February day, but that day it took. I was marked! Looking back, that frigid experience unlocked a passion that continues to burn in my heart today. I was on a new path. Baptism is not simply a ceremonial act but a pledge towards God. It is a symbol of what has occurred in the heart and life of a believer, but it is also a commitment to share Him with the world.

Some say, "I don't see the big deal; you don't have to be baptized to go to heaven." I agree you don't have to. While you can indeed go to heaven without being water baptized, you can go to hell with one. It's not a heaven or hell question; it's a declaration of your faith and commitment as a Christian.

Become a follower of Jesus, get baptized, and get involved in your local church. The power of each moment of your journey provides momentum for the next step.

CHAPTER FOUR

Holy Spirit

*

"This promise is to you, to your children, and to those far away."
- The Apostle Peter

Living the Christian life is sometimes easier said than done. The early days of my journey were quite challenging. Overcoming what was a lifetime of experiences, none of which had anything to do with faith. I'm now walking on a new path but not necessarily absent of old desires. Let me give a disclaimer before I continue. Everyone's path to freedom in Christ is different. Some people find immediate deliverance from their past addictions and desires, while others walk it out, unhinging themselves from one thing at a time. Don't allow yourself to use a person's struggle towards freedom as an excuse to continue your previous behavior, nor let someone's miraculous freedom cause you to doubt your journey. It is not a one-size-fits-all path.

For me, the freedom that I experienced when I was born again didn't come with an instant deliverance of my desire for drugs. I was instantly saved and placed on a new path that I would walk out. Coping with some of the larger addictions in my life was challenging. For example, when my feet hit the floor in the morning, I was thinking of cocaine and crack. I had to deal with that desire. My faith had not yet grown to a place in which it was a weapon I could use to overcome them. So, I used other medicinal means to cope with the urges.

However, I stayed faithful on the path, and one by one, I walked away from them. There came a day when I no longer had an urge for cocaine. Instead, I had a disdain for it. Soon after, I would let go of the crutch of marijuana. Then, it would be cigarettes.

As my faith grew, so did my strength.

Yours will, too! But, like me, you're going to need additional help!

A NEW STANDARD

You will hear people talk about the Old Testament as the law or rules we are no longer under. They are right to this extent; we no longer find our right standing with God by adhering to the 613 commandments given to Moses in the first five books of the Old Testament, often referred to as the Torah or Law. And they'll point to, rightfully so, the grace we have received in Christ, which was not based upon obeying commandments to be made right but by placing our faith in Him. (Ephesians 2:8). No argument there! But it doesn't render the Old Testament irrelevant either.

There are many commandments given in the Old Testament that are necessary to abide by in order to properly live the Christian life. Thou shall not have any other Gods, don't make idols, don't take God's name in vain, honor your parents, thou shall not steal, thou shall not kill, thou shall not lie about other people, thou shall not commit adultery, thou shall not covet your neighbor's belongings. That's nine of the ten commandments. As a Christian, you certainly agree that all of them are important to our lifestyle and must reflect Jesus. The point is this: while they are still relevant, we are not saved because we do them; we do them because we are saved.

There's an obvious difference between the relationship Israel had with God in the Old Testament and the one that we have in the New Testament. But if you're asking me, the requirement of living a fully devoted life to Christ from a New Testament standard is a higher level of living. Jesus raised the level from early on in His ministry. In His famous sermon on the mount in Matthew 5-7, He said, "You must not commit adultery." He's quoting one of the Ten Commandments in the

Old Testament. Then he says, "But I say, anyone who even looks at a woman with lust has already committed adultery with her in his heart." Now, He's introducing a New Testament standard.

I bet you would agree that abstaining from the actual act of being physically intimate with someone other than your spouse is easier to follow than just thinking about it. Jesus primarily says that if you're thinking about it, then it's already in your heart, and you are an adulterer. What an impossible standard. Yes, I have received grace. Yes, I have been saved. Yes, I have been baptized, but now my public and private life must be lived on this level. That seems impossible!

Jesus knew we didn't have the strength and courage to follow His footsteps. Therefore, He gave us the same strength and boldness He had—the Holy Spirit. Immediately rising out of the baptismal waters, the Holy Spirit took the lead over Jesus' life. First and foremost, He would lead Him to the wilderness. Matthew 4:1 (NLT) "Then Jesus was led by the Spirit into the wilderness to be tempted there by the devil."

Think of that! The Holy Spirit led Jesus to a wilderness to be tempted by the devil. After the 40 days in the wilderness had ended, Jesus would now walk in the power of the Holy Spirit. Luke 4:14 (NLT) "Then Jesus returned to Galilee, filled with the Holy Spirit's power. Reports about him spread quickly through the whole region."

We learned two great things from Jesus's relationship with the Holy Spirit. One, with the help of the Holy Spirit, we can overcome all temptations. Secondly, we are empowered by the Holy Spirit to live a supernatural life. Learning to conquer your flesh will be the first challenge, but with the help of the Holy Spirit, you will succeed. Day by day, you will get stronger. The more control the Holy Spirit has over you, the more He'll use you to help others.

THE DIVINE REPLACEMENT

Before His crucifixion and resurrection, Jesus prepared the disciples for His departure. To comfort them, He told them that the Holy Spirit would come. The Holy Spirit would be Jesus's divine replacement.

Jesus said not only would the Holy Spirit walk with them as He had, but He would also dwell inside of them.

> John 14:16–17 (NLT) "And I will ask the Father, and he will give you another Advocate, who will never leave you. He is the Holy Spirit, who leads into all truth. The world cannot receive him, because it isn't looking for him and doesn't recognize him. But you know him, because he lives with you now and later will be in you."

Jesus communicates this moment with a sense of urgency. He knew the Holy Spirit would be necessary for the disciples to carry on His ministry. If we intend to grow as followers of Jesus and live in His example, we'll need the same Spirit they had, the Holy Spirit!

THE TRANSITION

The Book of Acts is usually described in one of two ways. The Acts of the Apostles or the Acts of the Holy Spirit. I think it's both—the Acts of the Apostles through the Action of the Holy Spirit. The Book of Acts serves as a transition from the ministry of Jesus here on earth to the church's launch. In His final discourse, Jesus encourages the disciples to wait in Jerusalem until they have been endued with power. Luke 24:49 (NLT) "And now I will send the Holy Spirit, just as my Father promised. But stay here in the city until the Holy Spirit comes and fills you with power from heaven." He was telling them to wait until they got the promise before they started doing the ministry. That promise is the Holy Spirit.

It is fascinating that the eleven remaining guys had witnessed all the miracles Jesus performed. They heard all the teachings that He released to humanity. Yet, they needed the power that only comes from the Holy Spirit if they had any chance of succeeding. Every follower of Jesus, including you and me, needs the Holy Spirit.

A clear example is two stories involving Peter. His first position was the night in which Jesus would be arrested. He was being confronted by others who were questioning him concerning his relationship with

Jesus. He would deny any affiliation with Jesus three times, the final time cursing to prove that he was not a follower of Jesus (Luke 22:55-62). The next story is in The Book of Acts, chapter 2. Peter stands up amid a hostile environment where his life is under threat, and yet, with all boldness, he proclaims the name of Jesus. This was the first gospel message preached to a lost world after the resurrection. What was the difference? The baptism of the Holy Spirit!

The Holy Spirit would come demonstratively as the disciples waited in Jerusalem for this Promise. It happened fifty days after the resurrection on the Day of Pentecost. Pentecost, which means the fiftieth, is a Jewish Holy Day. The event is described in Acts 2:2–4 (NLT)

> "Suddenly, there was a sound from heaven like the roaring of a mighty windstorm, and it filled the house where they were sitting. Then, what looked like flames or tongues of fire appeared and settled on each of them. And everyone present was filled with the Holy Spirit and began speaking in other languages, as the Holy Spirit gave them this ability."

The Holy Spirit came roaring in and filled all the 120 gathered believers, and immediately, their language changed. Many different nationalities were gathered in Jerusalem at the time due to the Holy Day, and they all heard the beautiful things of God in their language. Acts 2:7–8 (NLT) "They were completely amazed. "How can this be?" they exclaimed. "These people are all from Galilee, and yet we hear them speaking in our own native languages!"

The Holy Spirit took Jesus' disciples and made them Apostles. The word apostle means 'sent ones' (Logos Library System). Jesus sent the Apostles with the power of the Holy Spirit to preach the gospel to the lost (Matthew 28:19-20). The church was born, and the day ended with three thousand people accepting Jesus as Lord and Savior. Those who were saved became disciples. That's the way it works! Acts 2:41–42 (NKJV) "Then those who gladly received his word were baptized; and that day about three thousand souls were added to them. And they continued steadfastly in the apostles' doctrine and fellowship, in the breaking of bread, and in prayers."

HE'S PERSONAL

The role of the Holy Spirit operates very personally with us. One of His intentions is to cultivate our character to reflect Jesus. His voice will continually correct and direct us through the journey. Jesus describes that aspect of His role like this in John 16:8 (NLT) "And when he comes, he will convict the world of its sin, and of God's righteousness, and of the coming judgment."

That's right, His voice will point out things you should do and those you shouldn't. Some things will be about sinful behavior, and others will be about building your witness. For example, before you open your mouth to lie, He'll be shouting loud inside of you, "Don't tell that lie." Or after you lie, He'll remind you that you just lied, and you'll know it.

At this point, you must respond to Him. You must acknowledge the error and repent. Sometimes, it may even require going back and setting the record straight with whom you lied to or about. Your response demonstrates your surrender to the leadership of the Holy Spirit. Romans 8:13–14 (NKJV) "For if you live according to the flesh you will die; but if by the Spirit you put to death the deeds of the body, you will live. For as many as are led by the Spirit of God, these are sons of God."

Again, everything is not just about sin.

Influence is the key to moving people. The Apostle Paul uses an extreme example to illustrate that even if something is not sinful it can be harmful. 1 Corinthians 8:9 (NLT) "But you must be careful so that your freedom does not cause others with a weaker conscience to stumble."

To add context, he said if you're a firm believer and know that there is only one true God and you have an opportunity to share a meal where the meat came from an offering to an idol, eat it up; it is just meat. However, he adds a disclaimer: if someone sees you eating and doesn't understand that it is just meat, they are likely to assume you are partaking in idolatry by eating.

They could conclude that it is ok to participate in idolatry or view you as someone who compromises. Either way, your witness will be ineffective, and their life will be impacted negatively. He concluded by saying don't eat it. It's not about sin. It's about representing Jesus. Don't try to use something as not being sinful as your right to indulge. Consider the impact. Be concerned about how others see you. The Holy Spirit will raise awareness in you to ensure you can reach others with the gospel. This is called being led by the Holy Spirit; just like He led Jesus through the wilderness. He will also lead you through every circumstance or situation you face.

HE'S A GUIDE

The Holy Spirit is the divine guide to truth. When Jesus was being tested in the wilderness, the key to His success was using the scripture. The devil would tempt Him by using scripture out of context, and Jesus would use scripture in context to push back. Matthew 4:6–7 (NKJV) "and said to Him, "If You are the Son of God, throw Yourself down. For it is written: 'He shall give His angels charge over you,' and, 'In their hands they shall bear you up, Lest you dash your foot against a stone.' " Jesus said to him, "It is written again, 'You shall not tempt the LORD your God.' "

The devil quotes a portion of Psalms 91, but Jesus knows the truth in scripture and responds with Deuteronomy 6:16.

Jesus taught many things that the disciples did not understand until they were baptized in the Holy Spirit (John 12:16). In John 16:13 (NLT) "When the Spirit of truth comes, he will guide you into all truth…" It is the Holy Spirit's responsibility to reveal God's intentions in the scriptures. He will cause you to understand what you read in scripture so that you can apply it to your life and share it with others.

A good example is when Philip came upon the Ethiopian man who was reading scripture and couldn't understand. Acts 8:29–31 (NLT) "The Holy Spirit said to Philip, "Go over and walk along beside the carriage." Philip ran over and heard the man reading from the prophet Isaiah. Philip asked, "Do you understand what you are reading?" The man replied, "How can I, unless someone instructs me?" And he urged

Philip to come up into the carriage and sit with him."

Philip, who had encountered the truth of Jesus earlier, would explain the passage and lead the man to give his life to Jesus.

You and I will grow in understanding scripture as the Holy Spirit guides us to its truth. Don't be intimidated when you read the bible. Don't say, "I don't understand". Invite the Holy Spirit to guide you. As you understand the truth, it will produce freedom in you and others (John 8:32).

HE EMPOWERS

One of the last statements from Jesus concerning the baptism in the Holy Spirit is in Acts 1:8 (NKJV) "But you shall receive power when the Holy Spirit has come upon you; and you shall be witnesses to Me in Jerusalem, and in all Judea and Samaria, and to the end of the earth."

I want to highlight the word 'witness' in the original Greek language from the verse. The word is *'martus'* (Logos Library System). It means demonstrating what you've seen and heard before others as truth, like being a witness in a court hearing. We get our English word 'martyr' from this word. A martyr is someone who dies for what they believe. The Holy Spirit helps us die to ourselves so that we may tell the world about Jesus!

The Holy Spirit will use you to capture the world's attention. In Acts chapter 3, the apostles are going to a prayer meeting at the temple. As they approached the door, a lame man was sitting by the door, begging for money. Look what happens in Acts 3:4–7 (NKJV)

> "And fixing his eyes on him, with John, Peter said, "Look at us." So he gave them his attention, expecting to receive something from them. Then Peter said, "Silver and gold I do not have, but what I do have I give you: In the name of Jesus Christ of Nazareth, rise up and walk." And he took him by the right hand and lifted him up, and immediately his

feet and ankle bones received strength."

When the Holy Spirit comes into our lives, we receive power and supernatural abilities. This supernatural power validates the authenticity of the gospel message. As everyone witnessed this man being healed, their curiosity was provoked, and they asked, "How?" Peter and John would take full advantage of the moment and lead five thousand people to Jesus (Acts 4:4). One man was healed, and God used it to confirm that Jesus is the Messiah.

From that day forward the church experienced many wonderful acts by the Holy Spirit. Acts 4:33 (NKJV) "And with great power the apostles gave witness to the resurrection of the Lord Jesus. And great grace was upon them all."

That work continues today through you and me. Trust the Holy Spirit in you to be bold and courageous in your encounters with others.

THE NEXT STEP

The Holy Spirit is the gift from God. Every follower of Jesus needs to take the next step and receive the baptism of the Holy Spirit. How do you receive the Holy Spirit? Simple, you ask! After listening to the Apostle Peter preach his first message in the power of the Holy Spirit, the audience asked him, "...Men and brethren, what shall we do?" Acts 2:37 (NKJV). Peter told them to turn to Jesus and get baptized and "...you shall receive the gift of the Holy Spirit." Acts 2:38 (NKJV)

Jesus said our heavenly Father will give the Holy Spirit to anyone who asks, "...how much more will your heavenly Father give the Holy Spirit to those who ask Him!" Luke 11:13 (NKJV)

Say a prayer today, "Father, I want the Holy Spirit; baptize me in your Holy Spirit."

Don't talk yourself out of the need for the Holy Spirit. None of us can live the life of faith to the fullest without the Holy Spirit. Acts 2:39 (NKJV) "For the promise is to you and to your children, and to all who are afar off, as many as the Lord our God will call."

The Holy Spirit will help us live fully devoted to Jesus. You cannot do it on your own. Don't try! The world needs your witness!

Remember, the only Jesus that the world will see is the Jesus they see in you and me. The Holy Spirit will make sure they see Him through you!

CHAPTER FIVE

Discipleship Habits

*

"Discipline is choosing between what you want now and what you want most."
-Abraham Lincoln

George "Shotgun" Shuba played baseball for the Brooklyn Dodgers in the 1950s. He was the first National League player to hit a pinch-hit home run in a World Series game. In his book, The Boys of Summer, which chronicled the Brooklyn Dodgers of the 1950s, Roger Kahn describes the swing of George "Shotgun" Shuba, a bench player, as being "so compact that it appeared as natural as a smile." ("George Shuba").

When Kahn mentions this to Shuba, he is unimpressed. He took Kahn to the basement, where he had baseball bats filled with lead. Then, he pulled out a notebook and described his "natural" swing as the result of 600 swings a night, 4,200 swings a week, and 46,200 swings every winter, all using an extra-heavy 44 oz. bat. "You call that natural?" Shuba said (Posnanski).

What may look to others as "natural as a smile" came with discipline.

George Shuba's discipline put him at bat in the World Series. God intends to use your life similarly. He wants to put you up to bat in the

41

critical game we call life. As you and I follow Jesus, it will take the same discipline to deliver in the moment. George's discipline made him a baseball player. Our discipline makes us disciples. Our walk with Jesus must become as "natural as a smile."

There are three critical disciplines to living as a disciple: The Word, prayer, and worship.

THE WORD

My desire to grow in my faith was enormous when I first got saved. I completely immersed myself in pursuing a better understanding of the redemption story in the Bible. If a church service was happening in my area, I would go. When I came home from work, I would go into the bedroom, get my Bible out, and read it. Every night, when I lay down to sleep, I put the Bible on cassette tapes in the player and listened until I fell asleep. Did I understand everything I was reading? Of course not! Neither will you in the beginning. For me, I called it getting lost in the stories. I enjoyed reading about the journey of faith of those in the Bible: their struggles, temptations, challenges, and triumphs. I could find something about me in each story. Best of all, I saw how God worked through it all, which increased my faith. If He did it for them, He will do it for me.

As a born-again follower of Jesus, you need nourishment. The Apostle Peter puts it this way in 1 Peter 2:2 (TPT) "In the same way that nursing infants cry for milk, you must intensely crave the pure spiritual milk of God's Word. For this "milk" will cause you to grow into maturity, fully nourished and strong for life."

Babies need nourishment. Instinctively, they cry out for it. They do not know the value of it; they don't know the ingredients in the milk. They don't even know the name of the drink they are drinking. One thing for sure is they stop crying when they get it. The more spiritual milk you get, the less crying you will do about life circumstances.

Growing is about taking in nourishment and then learning to take steps. Just read, and as you do, you'll develop an overall sense of the Biblical narrative. This will pay huge dividends as you start discovering your role within the body of Christ. For instance, let's say one day, you'll lead a group discussion on a particular subject. As you open your bible to prepare, you'll be amazed at the various stories in the bible that come to mind without even going to the passage. This experience will not only amaze you but give you great confidence.

Secondly, I cannot tell you the times I've been speaking to someone, and out of my mouth comes this biblical story with a principle attached that I never even thought of before. There have been many times I've thought, "I have no idea where that came from." However, that is exactly how the Holy Spirit works. John 14:26 (NLT) "But when the Father sends the Advocate as my representative—that is, the Holy Spirit—he will teach you everything and will remind you of everything I have told you."

The Holy Spirit will pull out of you what you have put inside, like a checking account. He will withdraw your deposits. If you make no deposits, He cannot make withdrawals. Get lost in the stories of the Bible.

WINNING THE BATTLE INSIDE

Let me add one more thing about the power of the Bible. Not only does it guide us into a deeper understanding of who God is and His plans for humanity, but the Word is also an explorer in our hearts. The biggest battle you will face in your faith journey is you. You will need to be conquered. Your old habits, mindsets, desires, and dreams must be reckoned with. The word of God is the sword that helps you win the battle.

While it is true that many things will not be evident to you when you begin to read, there will be some scriptures you will understand immediately. These discoveries will be principles of conduct that cut away the old you and bring out the new. The word of God is designed to bring distinction between you and the world, between what is right in God's eyes and what is not.

Hebrews 4:12 (NLT) "For the word of God is alive and powerful. It is sharper than the sharpest two-edged sword, cutting between soul and spirit, between joint and marrow. It exposes our innermost thoughts and desires." Like a knife, the word of God will cut between right and wrong.

This cutting happens on the inside of you where your thoughts and desires are confused or even stuck in yesterday's habits and experiences. The word of God will go one by one, cutting away at your flesh and empowering your spirit. We call the process transformation. Romans 12:2 (NLT) "Don't copy the behavior and customs of this world, but let God transform you into a new person by changing the way you think. Then you will learn to know God's will for you, which is good and pleasing and perfect."

Changing the way you think changes the way you live.

PRAYER

The New Testament was originally written in Greek, and the Old Testament was originally written in Hebrew. Understanding the deeper meanings of the words in the translations of the Bible we read requires going back to the original language used. The Greek word for prayer is *proseuchomai* (Logos Library System). Proseuchomai means to come face-to-face with God and speak.

When we pray, we come face-to-face with God. Prayer is a dialogue with our creator. It is not a monologue where you drop off your request and walk away. Jesus said, "Ask and He will answer" (Matthew 7:7–8). Learn to pause when praying. Be still and give the Father space to speak. Pay close attention to the inner responses.

To follow Jesus means we follow His teachings, example, character, and motives. I believe that Jesus' success was tied to His prayer life. Look at the following scriptures.

- Matthew 14:23 (NKJV) "And when He had sent the multitudes away, He went up on the mountain by Himself to pray. Now when evening came, He was alone there."

- Mark 1:35 (NKJV) "Now in the morning, having risen a long while before daylight, He went out and departed to a solitary place; and there He prayed."

- Luke 5:15–16 (NKJV) "However, the report went around concerning Him all the more; and great multitudes came together to hear, and to be healed by Him of their infirmities. So He Himself often withdrew into the wilderness and prayed."

- Luke 6:12 (NKJV) "Now it came to pass in those days that He went out to the mountain to pray, and continued all night in prayer to God."

Jesus was a man of prayer. Indeed, the disciples saw a connection between Jesus' private devotion and His public presentation. Jesus described the power of prayer in Matthew 6:6 (NKJV) "But you, when you pray, go into your room, and when you have shut your door, pray to your Father who is in the secret place; and your Father who sees in secret will reward you openly."

The conversations in your private prayers will have a public presentation.

The disciples were so moved that they asked Jesus to teach them to pray.

Luke 11:1–4 (NKJV) "Now it came to pass, as He was praying in a certain place, when He ceased, that one of His disciples said to Him, "Lord, teach us to pray, as John also taught his disciples." So He said to them, "When you pray, say: Our Father in heaven, Hallowed be Your name. Your kingdom come. Your will be done On earth as it is in heaven. Give us day by day our daily bread. And forgive us our sins, For we also forgive everyone who is indebted to us. And do not lead us into temptation, But deliver us from the evil one.""

We could spend hours breaking down this prayer model from Jesus.

Let me point out two things. One, we pray to the Father in the name of Jesus. Jesus said direct your prayers to your heavenly Father "When you pray, say: Our Father in heaven". He then teaches us in John 14:13 (NKJV) "And whatever you ask in My name, that I will do, that the Father may be glorified in the Son."

Prayer is like a checking account. God owns the bank. The account is in Jesus' name. You and I simply get the checkbook. When we write the check (pray), we take it to our Father to cash (answer). The signature on the check is Jesus', not yours. You're not banking on your name. You are counting on His name! You can never overdraft His account. He said, "Whatsoever you ask in my name." After every prayer, end it with, "I ask this in Jesus' name. Amen." or simply "In Jesus' name, amen."

The word amen means, so be it (Logos Library System). When you finish your prayer say 'amen', then walk away believing. Jesus said in Mark 11:24 (NKJV) "Therefore I say to you, whatever things you ask when you pray, believe that you receive them, and you will have them."

Prayer is the place to receive.

Secondly, the purpose of prayer is to bring heaven's will to earth, "Your kingdom come. Your will be done. On earth as it is in heaven." Prayer is like a conduit that allows God's intention to become Earth's reality. Reading the scriptures, as described, gets God's word inside of you. This transformation changes your desires and aligns your will with God. Your life now becomes a place where God accesses the world around you through you. God uses your prayer life as one point of access. Look at how the Apostle John describes it:

> 1 John 5:14–15 (NKJV) "Now this is the confidence that we have in Him, that if we ask anything according to His will, He hears us. And if we know that He hears us, whatever we ask, we know that we have the petitions that we have asked of Him."

Knowing God's plan for your life and the world around you must be a part of your prayer life. Sure, prayer is where I share my needs with

God. It is a place I ask for and believe in a better life for my family and me. But remember, your needs and future are connected to God's will and purpose. When you pray His will, it will keep you tied to His purpose, which now has become yours.

PRAY WITHOUT CEASING

Smith Wigglesworth was a British Evangelist in the early to mid-twentieth century. During his ministry, he saw unbelievable miracles occur. People were healed of every kind of sickness. Physical deformities were miraculously restored. There are even records of someone raised from the dead. Could you imagine such? People came from all over the world to be in his meetings. Someone once asked him how much time he spent in prayer each day. Assuming that he must pray hours each day for God to use him in such a mighty way. Wigglesworth surprised the man by saying, "I never pray for more than fifteen minutes at a time. . . but I never go more than fifteen minutes without praying" ("Smith Wigglesworth Quotes").

Prayer is a lifestyle of fellowship with God. Sure, you and I should set aside extended times of prayer. But we don't wait to pray. 1 Thessalonians 5:17 states, " Never stop praying." (NLT). The writer is saying to live connected to God with prayer. Prayers can be shouted, whispered, or internal. It's not about volume. Prayer can be hours or seconds. It's not about time. Prayer is about faith!

As your day moves and a person or situation comes to mind, pause and say a short prayer. For example, if someone you know may be sick, take a moment and say something like this: "Father, I pray that you heal John in Jesus' name." Then move on. When you pray, you are showing your reliance on God and inviting Him into the situation.

WORSHIP

King David is an Old Testament King from whom God said the Messiah Jesus would come. He is described by God Himself as a man after God's heart (1 Samuel 13:14). There are many reasons for the relationship of gratitude between God and David. God uses David to save a flock of sheep by killing a lion and a bear (1 Samuel 17:36).

There is an extraordinary feat of the teenage David killing Goliath with a slingshot (1 Samuel 17:49). The list goes on and on of how God saved, protected, fed and led David. However, I believe it was His worship that captured the attention of God.

David wrote songs, played an instrument, and would dance before the Lord with all His might (2 Samuel 6:45). A mighty warrior would find his success in worshipping the one who made it all possible. The presence of God in David's life was the most sought-after desire (Psalms 22:3).

The final discipline of discipleship is worship. The Word of God weaponizes you. Prayer is a divine exchange: You ask, and God provides. Worship is your way of saying thank you. It is a vocal and physical expression of your love, appreciation, adoration, and your gratitude.

Three words are often used to describe God: He is omnipotent, meaning all-powerful; omniscient, meaning all-knowing; and omnipresent, meaning present everywhere at all times. Like David, you will grow to see Him in your life in these various ways. His power will appear in different events in your life. At times, it will be miraculous, unexplainable, like killing giants. This will expand your boundaries and make you believe in what others call impossible. His words will guide you to your purpose. You will see He knows everything; nothing surprises Him. You will learn to trust His leadership. You will feel his presence in both difficult times and joyful moments. You will learn to sense His proximity and grow in confidence no matter what you are facing, knowing you are not alone. Worship will be the consequence of this growing relationship. You will learn to sing and dance!

ATMOSPHERE CHANGER

I love Psalm 22:3 (NKJV) "But You are holy, Enthroned in the praises of Israel."

This verse conveys the idea that when you start worshipping the Lord, He places His throne on top of your praise. Worship has the power to change atmospheres when God's presence shows up. In 1 Samuel 16, young David is anointed as the next king of Israel. The current king was under a spiritual attack. One of his servants mentioned this sixteen-year-old kid named David to him. They told King Saul that when David worshipped, it changed the atmosphere. So Saul calls for David to lead praise and worship at his palace. One day, an evil spirit is tormenting Saul. David, over in the corner, starts playing his instrument and singing to the Lord. Look what happened in 1 Samuel 16:23 (NLT) "And whenever the tormenting spirit from God troubled Saul, David would play the harp. Then Saul would feel better, and the tormenting spirit would go away."

Read that verse again! As David worshipped, this evil spirit had to flee. Why? David built a place for God's presence to rest. There is no way you can be tormented in the presence of the Lord. Worship is truly a weapon.

You don't have to be in church to get into the right atmosphere. You can change an atmosphere wherever you're willing to worship. Worship must become part of your lifestyle. Give God the glory for all His wonderful works in your life. Praise Him for what He has done and what He will do. Worship will change the atmosphere in your home, car, or work. As you just read, it will also help others who are in the presence of your worship. The scripture didn't say Saul worshipped. He was a beneficiary of the atmosphere worship created. When you worship, your family will benefit as well.

WE ARE HIS INSTRUMENTS

Worship is physical. Some people will raise their hands and close their eyes. Some will clap their hands. Others may jump up and down, bow on their knees, or lay on the ground. Some may even cry. All of these are expressions of their relationship with God and are biblical. Look at these scriptures:

- Psalm 47:1 (NLT) "Come, everyone! Clap your hands! Shout to God with joyful praise!"

- Psalm 95:6 (NLT) "Come, let us worship and bow down. Let

us kneel before the LORD our maker..."

- Psalm 134:2 (NLT) "Lift your hands toward the sanctuary and praise the LORD."

Worship is vocal. Songs give lyrics and sounds to say what's in our hearts and to express our love for God physically. Sometimes, what I feel doesn't come with the right words. Songs give us the words that describe what we are feeling. There are numerous songs written in your Bible. As a matter of fact, the book of Psalms (songs) is 150 songs written to praise and worship God. The Bible encourages us to sing. Look at Psalm 98:1 (NLT) "Sing a new song to the LORD, for he has done wonderful deeds. His right hand has won a mighty victory; his holy arm has shown his saving power!"

We are encouraged to use the melodies of instruments; look at Psalm 150:3–4 (NLT) "Praise him with a blast of the ram's horn; praise him with the lyre and harp! Praise him with the tambourine and dancing; praise him with strings and flutes!"

Our God deserves to be worshipped.

Let everything that has breath praise the Lord (Psalms 150:6). God made you a musical instrument of praise. You have percussion—hands that clap and feet that stomp. You have a stringed instrument called vocal cords. You have a wind instrument called a windpipe. With every breath, your instrument has the capacity to worship God. As God works in your life and reveals Himself to you, let it create a sound or a song of praise, thanksgiving, and admiration. Worship is the attitude of gratitude.

FINAL THOUGHT

Don't allow one way of worship to become your box. Seasons change, and so do our experiences with God. Your worship should grow as your perspective of Him grows.

Maintain a consistent prayer life. Get face-to-face with God and have conversations that empower you to walk in His purpose. These private conversations will have public consequences. The world needs to see you after you've been face-to-face with Him.

Allow God's word to sort you and the world around you out. It will cut away the confusion and bring distinction to the who, what, when, where, and how of being a fully devoted follower of Jesus. Believe His word over all others.

These three critical disciplines ensure you stay on the discipleship pathway, and staying disciplined will prepare you for your next step- and there is a next step! This is a lifetime journey towards meeting Jesus again!

SECTION TWO

Elementary Principles

Hebrews 6:1–3 (NKJV) "Therefore, leaving the discussion of the elementary principles of Christ, let us go on to perfection, not laying again the foundation of repentance from dead works and of faith toward God, of the doctrine of baptisms, of laying on of hands, of resurrection of the dead, and of eternal judgment. And this we will do if God permits."

CHAPTER SIX

Another Step

*

"True spiritual maturity is the consistent practice of elementary principles."
- Damon Thompson

The hardest people to convince are those closest to you, especially if they have been collateral damage to your pre-Jesus life. My family stood as spectators early on in my journey with Christ. But as time passed, my influence began to change drastically. Now, I wasn't the one they were praying for; they were coming to me for prayer. Instead of offering me "get my life right" advice when I saw them, they asked me for insight. Why? My lifestyle was demonstrating my spiritual growth.

Circumstances cannot determine the health of your journey. When everything goes your way, you live high on the mountain. But when life hits you in the gut, you fall into the valley of despair. This type of instability will not only harm your spiritual health but also your influence. As I've mentioned before, my life was a wreck. When I accepted Jesus, I was the one who changed, my circumstances remained the same. However, I maintained pursuit, and I stayed consistent. A year or so later, my brother came to me while going through some of his own challenges. He said to me, "I want the peace you have." He had witnessed life continuing to throw its punches at my wife and me, but he also witnessed our faithfulness to the journey.

You will win the day as your relationship deepens with the Lord.

OLD HABITS DIE HARD, NEW ONES ARE THE SWORD THAT KILLS THEM

Growing in Christ is not only about consumption but also about application. Jesus said in John 8:32 (NKJV), "And you shall know the truth, and the truth shall make you free." Was He talking about just reading and understanding the truth? Was He implying that having a good understanding of the Bible would result in freedom? No! The word 'know' in the verse means 'come to know, to know by experience.' It is a Jewish idiom for sexual intercourse between a man and a woman. (Logos Library System). For example, in Genesis 4:1 (NKJV) "Now Adam knew Eve, his wife, and she conceived...."

Adam knew Eve, and she became pregnant. The word of God is like a seed, and our hearts are like a womb. When that seed is sown into our hearts, and we believe it to the extent we act on it, then the fruit is produced (Matthew 13:23). Let me say it like this: The word of God contains the promises from God. We access the promise by application. Therefore, my obedience unlocks the promise within its passages. I don't gain access by knowing the passage but by practicing the principles.

Should we consume the Bible? Should we expose ourselves to teachings as much as possible? Absolutely! However, consistent reinforcement of the foundational principles of your faith will ensure the proper allocation of the deeper truths upon which you build your life. New revelations are the building blocks of the life of faith, and elementary doctrines are the foundation on which they stand. With every new revelation, your faith will grow. As your faith grows, so does your influence. Why? Between your faith growing and your influence increasing, you will produce the fruit of a transformed life. Old habits will be displaced by a new way of living. This new way of living is the fruit; other people get to pull this fruit from the branches of your life and "taste and see that God is good (Psalms 34:8)." The result is the opportunity to gain influence in their life that helps lead them to greater freedom in Christ.

GOING DEEPER

When we begin reading the book of Hebrews, the writer shows the superiority of who Jesus is compared to Old Testament people. One of the purposes is to pull the church into a deeper understanding of scripture. One of the great benefits of being pulled in deeper is that God has more resources to pull out of you to share with the world around you. I dare to say that most of us are reluctant to share our faith, not because we don't love Jesus or we're not convinced about who He is. Maybe we're afraid of not having answers to the questions.

So, out of the gate, in Hebrews chapter 1, the writer tells them that Jesus is far superior to Angels. Why is he doing that? In the Old Testament, the word of God was mediated to humanity through angels (Hebrews 2:2). Therefore, angels were highly esteemed because of their mediation throughout the Old Testament. He wanted the readers to know that if they had put their confidence in what the angel said in the Old Testament, Jesus was superior to angels, and they should trust what He was saying more.

Moses, one of the most revered people in the Old Testament, was the guy who went into the mountain and received this word, brought it down to the Israelites, established the worship system, and built the Tabernacle. I mean, you watch a guy walk up a mountain, spend 40 days communing with God, and return with his face shining like light because of his proximity to the spirit of the Lord (Exodus 24:29-30). You're going to put him in a category all by himself.

So, in order to elevate Jesus above the mighty Moses, the writer compares them both by an illustration of a servant and a son. He said that Moses was a servant in the house. Serving the needs of the Father, our God, who owns the house. He then stated that Jesus is the Son whom God put over the house (Hebrews 3:5-6). This essentially states that the Son is greater than the servant and if you followed the servant in the Old Testament, you should definitely follow the Son in the New Testament.

The writer continues to emphasize Jesus's authority and power by contrasting Him to the religious icons of the Old Testament. This leads to a deeper understanding of who Jesus is and what His role must be in our lives. Consequently, our faith grows in Jesus!

YOU'RE NOT READY FOR THIS STEP

Moses established the priestly roles the Levitical tribe of Israel had carried out for 1500 years. They were still the mediators between God and the nation of Israel in Jesus' day. The priests stood as a bridge, some call an intercessor, between God and the people. He represented the people before God and God before the people. The top leader of the priesthood was the High Priest. Moses' brother Aron was the first High Priest in Israel. Every High Priest in scripture came from the family of Aron.

The writer of Hebrews passes over this comparison with little discussion and discusses a high priest barely mentioned in the Old Testament. A high priest not from the Levites and certainly not from Aron. Someone with very little knowledge written about him - Melchizedek. He was the priest and king of Jerusalem, called Salem, in the days of Abraham (Genesis 14:18). He is a type of Jesus in the Old Testament. Jesus is both our High Priest and King. While Melchizedek was not part of the Levitical priesthood, it was understood throughout Jewish history he represented someone to come (Psalms 110:4). However, no one associated him with the promised Messiah. This was about to be a big revelation that had been hidden.

Remember, the writer of Hebrews intended to help Jesus' followers gain a deeper understanding of Him through scripture.

Right when he's about to share this profound truth about Melchizedek, he stops. He recognizes that the Christian believers were not prepared. He lets them know it in Hebrews 5:11 (NLT) "There is much more we would like to say about this, but it is difficult to explain, especially since you are spiritually dull and don't seem to listen."

Talk about a hit. He's saying this is a deep revelation, and you are not ready for it. He doesn't leave them hanging, either. Here is how I know you aren't prepared: Hebrews 5:12 (NLT) "You have been believers for so long now that you ought to be teaching others. Instead, you need someone to teach you again the basic things about God's word. You are like babies who need milk and cannot eat solid food."

Wow! He says you have an infantile mindset towards the Kingdom. You're a baby, Christian. After all this time of following Jesus, you are still in the same place when you began. He's letting them know that God has deep truths to share from His word, but they "can't handle the truth." I couldn't resist the Few Good Men quote by Jack Nicholson. They could not hear the truth due to their spiritual immaturity.

MILK OR MEAT

God's word can be categorized in two ways. One, it's like 'milk.' The born-again believer needs the elementary principles of God's word to grow (1 Peter 2:2) which are foundational doctrines. They become core beliefs on which we build our life of faith. The other is called 'meat.' These are the concealed revelations of God's word for mature believers, such as the deeper truth concerning Melchizedek. These truths are often wrapped symbolically in the Old Testament scripture or metaphorically wrapped in a biblical narrative. To qualify for the meat, there has to be practical living demonstrated by the strength received from the milk. The fruit of maturity is identified in actively teaching and sharing your faith with others "...you ought to be teaching others..." (Hebrews 5:12).

As our attention spans decrease in a world overrun with information, we must not assume that an occasional platitude caught on our favorite social media outlet is enough. Fruit doesn't come from communication; fruit comes from the experience of living through it. You don't get it any other way. Walking with God requires understanding God's word and surrendering to the prompting of His Spirit to step out and trust what you know with action.

The beginning of your journey should focus on understanding these basic foundational doctrines of faith. Once you understand them, you should practice them. You prove by practice so that you can teach others. When you teach others, you position yourself to be taught deeper truths of the Christian life. You've heard the phrase, "Practice makes perfect!" God is not expecting you to be perfect, but He is looking for you to take the steps towards consistency. I like to say, "Consistency will grow into maturity!"

This next section will focus on six foundational doctrines of your Christian faith. These doctrines are the base on which you are to build your life of faith. Milk is great for growing, but meat puts muscle on your bones. God wants you to be a meat eater, but milk comes first. For example, when building a house, the foundation is first. You don't live in a foundation you live on it.

CHAPTER SEVEN

Repentance

*

"Of all acts of man, repentance is most divine. The greatest of all faults is to be conscious of none."
- Thomas Carlyle

Don't you just hate critics? You know, the judgmental people who constantly point out what's wrong with you. Those who try to make themselves look better at your expense. When people join the faith community, there is often a trepidation of being judged. All of a sudden, it appears your lifestyle is on full display, and you have to change it now, or you get a label from some judgmental church member. Hear this clearly: God accepts everyone just as they are. However, He will not leave you how He finds you. Change is a process that takes time for everyone. So don't beat yourself up or call it quits when you are just getting started. Furthermore, your critics should not be allowed to do so either.

As you grow in your relationship with God, you'll discover that there are some things He says that you won't agree with or even like. There are scriptures that I read I wish weren't in the Bible. For example, in Matthew 5:39, Jesus says "If someone slaps you on the right cheek, offer the other cheek also." As a father, I raised my son never to bully or start a fight. What I did encourage him to do was defend himself. I remember his first fight. While at school, he and another kid had a disagreement that resulted in some punches being thrown. We had been contacted about the situation. As a father, I must manage my emotions, be mature, and have the right conversation. Really, I just wanted to know two things. One, who started it? If that answer was "the other guy." I only wanted to know, "Who won?"

My instinct was not to reprimand him for not turning the other cheek. There are those scriptures! But, if I am going to start walking like Jesus, these principles must govern my character and conduct. When Jesus was arrested, He was hit in the face and yet restrained Himself (Matthew 26:67). He could have taken the guy out in a minute. How would we feel if the description of the event said, "A guy came and punched Jesus in the face, and then Jesus gave him a beat down"? We'd see Jesus a little bit differently, wouldn't we? Under the circumstances, we might give Him a pass, but it would redefine Him.

Agreeing with God is a foundational principle that must be wrestled out in our lives.

In the last chapter, we left off with the writer of Hebrews wanting to teach deeper spiritual truth to the Christians. But before he continued, he paused to point out that they were immature and needed to be taught again the foundational truths. These truths are pointed out in Hebrews 6:1–3 (NLT)

> "So let us stop going over the basic teachings about Christ again and again. Let us go on instead and become mature in our understanding. Surely we don't need to start again with the fundamental importance of repenting from evil deeds and placing our faith in God. You don't need further instruction about baptisms, the laying on of hands, the resurrection of the dead, and eternal judgment. And so, God willing, we will move forward to further understanding."

These six doctrines are not meant to spend your entire life trying to understand. They are foundational and gateways to your life journey as a follower of Jesus. If there is no clarity here, what you learn going forward will be filtered through a contaminated lens. A person learns through what they already know. When you read the Bible or listen to a sermon, your foundation determines how you process it and apply it to your life. Equally, what you tell others is the truth; depends on your foundation.

At the top of the list is repentance. Repentance is the catalyst for everything that God will build in your life. The very first message that comes to humanity in the New Testament is to repent. Matthew 3:1–2 (NLT) "In those days John the Baptist came to the Judean wilderness and began preaching. His message was, "Repent of your sins and turn to God, for the Kingdom of Heaven is near."

Following His baptism, Jesus picks up the message as well. Matthew 4:17 (NLT) "From then on Jesus began to preach, "Repent of your sins and turn to God, for the Kingdom of Heaven is near.""

When Jesus sent the disciples to witness, they called people to repent. Look here in Mark 6:12 (NLT) "So the disciples went out, telling everyone they met to repent of their sins and turn to God."

When the crowd heard the Apostle Peter preach the first message after Jesus ascended into heaven, their hearts were touched. They asked him what they should do, he said, "repent". Acts 2:37–38 (NLT) "Peter's words pierced their hearts, and they said to him and to the other apostles, "Brothers, what should we do?" Peter replied, "Each of you must repent of your sins and turn to God, and be baptized in the name of Jesus Christ for the forgiveness of your sins. Then you will receive the gift of the Holy Spirit."

Repentance is not a bad word Jesus uses. It's not a word He's trying to beat us up with. He's trying to grab our attention and build an expectation by saying the Kingdom of God is near. Repent is what you have to do to see the Kingdom clearly. Repent is what you're going to need to do to experience it. Always remember God has sought a relationship with you first. Repentance helps us see and experience the best of our relationship with God.

A CLEAR PERSPECTIVE

When I was younger, I thought that repentance meant saying I was sorry, asking God for forgiveness, and attending church more. I didn't understand until I was older that I was supposed to feel so strongly about sin that I would detest the idea of committing it. Sure, I felt remorse for my behavior, but it was more related to the consequences of my actions. Most of us wouldn't change until the consequences of our actions show up. So, when I was snorting cocaine, smoking crack, eating acid, smoking dope, drinking whiskey, and running on the roads, I was enjoying every minute of it. It wasn't until the consequences of the behavior started piling up, impacting my family and finances, that I was forced to make decisions. Some of us only change when we get caught. We only said we were sorry because somebody called us out, and we're trying to diffuse the situation.

Repentance is not simply asking God to forgive you. Repentance doesn't mean I'm sorry I did it. Repentance is not just feeling bad. Repentance is not saying I won't do it again.

Repentance is agreeing with God and turning to align with His will and ways. It is agreeing with how God feels about sin and with what God calls sin.

The Greek New Testament word for repentance is *"Metanoia."* (Logos Library System) It means "to change one's mind for the better, heartily to amend with abhorrence of one's past sins." Now, what am I supposed to change my mind to?

Remember, the scriptures previously shared said, "Repent of sin." In this context, metanoia is when you change your mind to the extent that you start agreeing with what God says about sin. Metanoia means I changed the way I see sin, and I see sin the way God sees sin. That's right; you are supposed to feel exactly how God feels about sin. If you and I feel the way God feels about sin, we will create more distance from sin by turning from it. Metanoia means that God has set a standard, and He calls out what is sin, and you agree with Him.

Repentance says, I've heard what God said, I agree, I changed my mind, and I'm now in unity with Him. When you turned to God, you gained access to the things of the Kingdom from God. They're freely made available to you. Some of you are in lack, even as followers of Jesus, because you don't practice repentance. I'm not saying you don't practice saying I'm sorry. I'm talking about owning what's going on to the extent that you say to yourself, "This is wrong, and I'm stopping it now." Instead of using excuses like, "I can't help it." Or "I'm just a sinner saved by grace." Or, "I'm only human." If you are not careful, you will make a whole list of excuses that justify wrong behavior and deny yourself access to these deeper spiritual truths that not only transform you but empower you to help others change their direction.

Luke, who wrote the book of Acts, said, "God overlooked people's ignorance about these things in earlier times, but now he commands everyone everywhere to repent of their sins and turn to him." (Acts 17:30 NLT).

Don't give yourself a pass with sin. The foundation of the kingdom is built on repentance. Don't treat sin as trivial or casual.

The Apostle Paul said in 2 Corinthians 7:10 (NLT) "For the kind of sorrow God wants us to experience leads us away from sin and results in salvation. There's no regret for that kind of sorrow. But worldly sorrow, which lacks repentance, results in spiritual death."

Did you read that? God wants you to experience sorrow when you sin. For godly sorrow leads and provokes us to repentance. He goes on to say that repentance causes us to experience the more profound results of our salvation.

We often don't feel broken over our sins. We don't allow remorse when we miss it or hurt somebody. I'm certainly not saying you will never miss the mark and sin again. I am saying repent: agree with God and return your life to the right path.

While this is foundational, it will be the most challenging—that is why it's number one on the list. You will find out God calls many behaviors we are comfortable with sin. You will be tempted to tear that page out. Don't do it! Choose to repent as you follow Jesus.

TEACHING REPENTANCE

We are called not only to understand the doctrine of repentance but also to teach others (Hebrews 5:12). This is where the rubber hits the proverbial road of sharing your faith with others. As shared in section one, sin is punishable by death. Jesus died to provide forgiveness for our sins and give us eternal life. If we effectively lead others to be fully devoted followers of Jesus, we can't avoid the primary roadblock: sin.

Remember, repent is not meant to be a bad word. Teaching others is not about getting the list of what the Bible calls sin out and telling people how wrong they are. No! Paul said in Romans 2:4 it's the "goodness of God that leads men to repentance". We come from a position of love and want the best for our friends, family, and strangers. After all that's what Jesus wants from us.

Penn Jillette from the famous magic duo Penn and Teller is a professed atheist. He tells a remarkable story of a man sharing his faith. After his show one evening, a man waited on the side to greet him. The man is very complimentary of Penn's showmanship and presentation. Penn said he was a gentleman, a businessman, and very kind. He said the man gave him a small Bible with an inscription on the front of it. He said he was quite sure the man knew that he was an atheist, yet he could feel his kindness in offering this gift. Penn said he has high respect for people who actually believe with all certainty that there is a heaven and hell and are willing to tell others, regardless of the social construct or the potential of being embarrassed. Penn asked, "How much do you have to hate a person not to tell them the truth?" He used an example: if you saw someone standing in the road and a truck was bearing down on them, would you not try to get them out of the road even if you had to tackle them? Of course we would! (beinzee).

Helping others see the truck about to run over them, which brings certain death, is everyone's call as a Christian. Showing them how to live devoted to Jesus is the best you have to offer. You can't help others be who God has called them to be if you disagree with what God calls sin. Even as a dad, teaching his son not to be a bully or start a fight seemed complete enough. But Jesus said turn the other cheek. Agreeing with God will challenge us in many areas of our life. It may not always make immediate sense to us. But once practiced, you'll experience the outcome and learn the truth, which makes us free.

The first stone of biblical doctrine we build on is repentance. Repentance cannot be a negotiable doctrine in your life. It cannot be subjective to cultural norms or moral acceptability. God defines what sin is. We agree with Him.

Sharing your faith is risky; not sharing it is eternally devastating for those who die lost. Jesus is coming! Repent for the kingdom is near!

CHAPTER EIGHT

Faith

*

"I believe in Christianity as I believe that the sun has risen: not only because I see it, but because by it I see everything else."
- C.S. Lewis

When I first got saved, it was all about gaining freedom from the life that previously held me captive. I was just trying to quit a lot of bad habits. I knew my behavior was destructive. For much of what I was doing, it didn't take scripture to change my mind. I was convinced. Most of the early part of our Christian walk involves quitting bad habits. Drinking, drugs, sex, smoking, cursing, lying, stealing, gossiping, and manipulation are all big problems. I could add many more things to the list. You get my point! There was no discussion concerning my purpose, where I should serve, or what church I should attend. First things first, let me get my life turned around. I need help; I'm not ready to help anyone else. At this point, I'm a taker, getting all I can in this new life.

As I turned more and more to God, it placed me on a new pathway. A road taking me from where He found me to eternity. But what about between here and there? Now I'm born again, baptized, and filled with the Holy Spirit. I read my Bible consistently, pray often, and attend worship gatherings. I repented of my sins and turned towards God.

The journey between here and eternity is called a walk of faith!

The second foundational doctrine is "faith in God." Hebrews 6:1 (NLT) "So let us stop going over the basic teachings about Christ again and again. Let us go on instead and become mature in our understanding. Surely we don't need to start again with the fundamental importance of repenting from evil deeds and placing our faith in God."

The definition of the word Faith in Greek is *"Pistis"*; it's the conviction that God exists and is the creator and ruler of all things, the provider and bestower of eternal salvation through Christ. (Logos Library System).

Faith is the now and the later of your walk. You need it now, and you'll need it later. It's the resource of trust and confidence in God that you can succeed no matter where He leads you or what He asks of you. Faith is the light that shines in darkness, saying, "This is going to end." Faith is the hope in your heart that what you do matters even if the change or impact is not evident. Faith is the lens you look out of when living. Faith says, "God, you are great, and I know it. And if I stay with you, it will work out just fine." Faith says what I see is temporary and subject to change.

When you put your complete trust and confidence in God, He responds. You will need faith for a personal situation you face, when someone is sick, a financial need, or a relationship need. It takes faith for everything.

GROWING FAITH

As a follower of Jesus, you will never find yourself walking with God and not need a measure of faith. So, the question for us should be, "If all of life requires faith, where does it come from, and how do I get more?" Faith comes from hearing God's word. Romans 10:17 (NKJV) "So then faith comes by hearing, and hearing by the word of God."

As I read God's word, the Holy Spirit validates its truth. From within, you'll feel it and be so sure of the truth that confidence will explode in your heart. For example, if you read the story in Matthew chapter 14 about Jesus walking on water, it grows your confidence in His power and ability. After all, He's heading towards His disciples stuck in a storm. After reading such a story, you gain confidence (faith) in Him concerning your own storms in life. You say to yourself, "If He has to walk on water to get to me, He will." You'll have a peace that says, "He knows where I am at all times."

As you continue to read, you discover Peter stepping out of the boat to walk towards Jesus. With his eyes fastened on Jesus, Peter walked on the water. Suddenly, the wind and waves get his attention. Turning his attention to the storm, Peter begins to sink. The hand of Jesus grabs him and leads him to safety. The story ends with Jesus teaching him about faith and doubt.

Here's the point: when you see Peter walking on the water in the storm, you not only grow in your confidence about the power and ability of Christ, but you grow in your faith as well. You know that if you step out with your eyes on Jesus, He'll protect and keep you too! You, too, can stand in the impossible situations of life. Faith was operating when Peter had his eyes on Jesus. Doubt was when he looked at the storm. It is the difference between standing and sinking. However, a bigger discovery is that even if I get my eyes off Him, His eyes are still on me.

Faith cannot rest solely on what you say you believe. It will require, at times, to get out of the boat to show it. The book of James describes it this way: James 2:26 (NLT) "Just as the body is dead without breath, so also faith is dead without good works."

What you do in every situation speaks to what you believe. I heard an old preacher say, "I read the Bible, then I act like I believe it." (Hagin). It won't always make sense; that's why you need faith.

You will not always have all your questions answered before you step out. But every time you step out, you'll find answers. Faith provides the courage and confidence to trust God so that you can keep walking on the path God has chosen.

INVISIBLE VISIBLE

We live in a tangible world. We believe what we see, right? We say things like "seeing is believing; I won't believe it until I see it." But that's not how it works in the life of faith. The unseen is the eternal reality God wants us to fixate on 2 Corinthians 4:18 (NLT) "So we don't look at the troubles we can see now; rather, we fix our gaze on things that cannot be seen. For the things we see now will soon be gone, but the things we cannot see will last forever."

This does not imply that what we face is not real, painful, or meaningless. Faith does not deny the reality of life. Faith doesn't deny that you are going through a difficult marriage. Faith doesn't deny the doctor's report. Faith says circumstances do not govern my mind, will, or emotions. Faith does not deny my challenges. It just looks at them differently through the lens of promise. It puts difficult circumstances in a temporary compartment. Hebrews 11:1 (NKJV) "Now faith is the substance of things hoped for, the evidence of things not seen."

Faith is like money! It has purchase power. It purchases hope, attitude, and outcomes. Faith buys your way out of the most challenging things life throws at you. Jesus didn't say to Peter, you only thought you were in a storm. Jesus was saying, keep your eyes on me in the storm, and you'll get through it.

"Doubt in your head does not keep faith from your heart"
- Kenneth Hagin

Peter heard the wind and felt the rain hitting him. He had to wipe the water from his eyes and feel the waves under his feet. He could smell the water and taste it. I guarantee you his five senses were fully alive, none of which Jesus addressed when they reached the safety of the boat. Jesus only says in Matthew 14:31 (NKJV), "O you of little faith, why did you doubt?" Here is a fact: it's possible to have doubt in your mind as you process the information your five senses are giving you while at the same time having faith in your heart as you are working through the situation. Your mind and heart will fight each other at times.

A man comes to Jesus in Mark chapter 9. His son is in complete torment and needs to be delivered. After several failed attempts by the disciples, he now stands before Jesus. Begging and pleading for his son, Jesus said this in Mark 9:23–24 (NKJV)

> Jesus said to him, "If you can believe, all things are possible to him who believes." Immediately the father of the child cried out and said with tears, "Lord, I believe; help my unbelief!"

This man's response describes the wrestling match we all face. It's like he's saying, I believe you can do it, but I'm not sure you'll do it for me. After all, he had already brought his son to the disciples; they could not help. Situations like this can deepen the doubt in your mind. Causing you to say, "Well, I tried, and nothing happened."

The way to win is by allowing faith to overthrow your doubt. The man didn't accept his son's situation even though his previous attempts failed. He kept pushing his belief over his unbelief. Let the heart win the battle over your mind. Keep pushing, keep believing. What you've been hoping for will come to pass! Present doubt cannot defeat a now faith! (Hebrews 11:1)

Faith requires a leap, a step, or a stand.

Indiana Jones is pursuing the Holy Grail, the cup of Christ. Battling the Nazis to reach it first, he finds himself in a desperate situation. His father has been shot, and the only thing that can save him is a drink from the cup of Christ. Armed with only a map in a book, he finds himself standing on one side of a cliff looking across a deep gorge at the other rock face with a cave opening. Looking down at the pages in the book, he realizes this moment is called the leap of faith from the lion's head. He closes his eyes, clutches the book to his chest, and takes a step. Rather than falling to his death, he lands on an invisible walkway across the gorge. He retrieves the cup and gives his father a drink, who is miraculously healed.

There will be times on this journey when you must close your eyes, cling to your Bible, and take the leap—putting your full confidence in

God. 2 Corinthians 5:7 (NLT) says, "For we live by believing and not by seeing."

The constant appeal of faith is to put my eyes on God, not my circumstances. Because if I put my eyes on God, I'll react differently to my circumstances. If I have my eyes on my circumstances, my emotion takes over, and I become emotionally expressive. Look at Peter; wherever His eyes went, so did his feelings. Faith determines whether you sink in the storm or stand on the water.

FAITH IN GOD

My daughter was going through a very difficult season in life. Her husband had just told her he wanted a divorce. They had been on a pathway to adopt three children. Her whole world seemed to fall apart as her husband walked out the door, and the DCS office came to pick up the children. She and I found ourselves sitting in a coffee shop as she was unpacking where she was. She told me that she did not know where her faith in God would be if she weren't able to see the adoption through. I told her that faith is not the tool that we get to use to change every circumstance in life to how we want it to be, but faith in God is the gift we have that says "no matter what circumstance we are facing in life, he is going to work all things out for the good" (Romans 8:28).

We are on a faith journey. Sure, there will be times when you feel like you are sinking and others when you are standing on the water in the midst of the storm. No matter where you are on the journey, it will require faith.

The second foundational stone for your life must be faith in God!

Faith is a foundational doctrine that must be laid in your life. It will keep you constant no matter the circumstances. When Peter got into the boat that day, it was under the direction of Jesus, who said, "Go to the other side." Jesus didn't promise a life without the storm, but we can always step out on His word. Whether getting in the boat and setting sail or walking on water during the storm. When it was all said and done, Peter anchored the boat on the other side, and you will, too. Have faith in God!

CHAPTER NINE

Baptisms and Laying on of Hands

*

"When I die, He arises, and then everything becomes possible."

I didn't have a say-so in which church I went to as a kid. I was raised by a single mom most of my life. She didn't even go to church when we were small kids. A bus from the local Baptist church would pick up kids in our neighborhood. When my mom found out, she arranged for us to ride to church on Sundays. Of course, she didn't go; I think she was looking for a break from the four kids. The children's ministry was having a contest to see who could bring the most visitors to the church. The winner would get a new bike. Now, we were very poor, and my sister wanted that bike. Week after week, my sister would round up the kids in the neighborhood. My mom had promised to go, but she made an excuse every week. It's the last Sunday to count your visitors, and my sister drags my mom from the bed to get on the bus. Reluctantly, my mom goes, and that morning, she gave her life to Jesus.

My sister won the bike that Sunday, but our family won a whole new lifestyle. My mom went all in with the life of faith. It wasn't long before we connected with my great-grandparents, whom we had never spent time with. They were Pentecostal Holiness people. My mom wanted to be around family while raising four kids We moved from the Baptist church to the United Pentecostal Church. I can tell you that

72

we were "no longer in Kansas" (Vidor, King et al). We moved from a relatively quiet conservative Baptist church to a highly emotional and very loud Pentecostal church. Not only was the style of worship different, but the beliefs were different, and the way faith was lived out and expressed was different, too.

I share this story because some of you may be like me, and the church you were raised in was not the one you chose. Consequently, how you see scripture may differ from that of others who were exposed to churches that differed from yours. This chapter is not about styles of worship or the better denomination. This book is about taking the steps to be a fully devoted follower of Jesus. We simply look to Jesus to define the correct doctrine (beliefs) and model them as an example.

THE TWO IN ONE

As we continue to ensure we have the proper foundations under us, let's talk about the next two doctrines the writer of Hebrews calls elementary principles: baptisms and laying on of hands.

> Hebrews 6:1–2 (NKJV) "Therefore, leaving the discussion of the elementary principles of Christ, let us go on to perfection, not laying again the foundation of repentance from dead works and of faith toward God, of the doctrine of baptisms, of laying on of hands, of resurrection of the dead, and of eternal judgment."

Each block of the foundational doctrines depends upon each other. For example, repentance from sin puts me on the pathway of a life of faith. The life of faith is expressed through baptisms and laying on of hands that lead me to resurrection and eternal judgment. Baptisms and the laying on of hands run together. One is empowering you, and the other is empowering others.

PLURAL NOT SINGULAR

The writer does not use the word baptism as in a single event; he uses the word baptisms as in multiple events. According to New Testament teachings, there are multiple baptisms, not just one. Jesus introduces these baptisms to His disciples before he leaves Acts 1:4–5 (NLT) "Once when he was eating with them, he commanded them, "Do not leave Jerusalem until the Father sends you the gift he promised, as I told you before. John baptized with water, but in just a few days you will be baptized with the Holy Spirit."

We discussed water baptism at length in chapter 3. So, I will only make a brief comment to remind you. First, water baptism is about public confession concerning your faith in Jesus. Second, it's about identifying with Him. Lastly, it is about commissioning you into the life of ministry as a follower of Jesus.

The second type of baptism is baptism in the Holy Spirit. In chapter four, we discussed the role of the Holy Spirit in cultivating our lives in holiness and influence. I want to take it one step further here. When baptized in the Holy Spirit, He brings spiritual gifting into your life. In 1 Corinthians 12, The Apostle Paul intends to educate the church on the spiritual gifts that the Holy Spirit gives us.

First, he informs us that we all have been given a gift to help others. 1 Corinthians 12:7 (NLT) "A spiritual gift is given to each of us so we can help each other."

Then, he goes on to point out nine of these gifts. They are often referred to as power gifts. 1 Corinthians 12:8–10 (NKJV) "For to one is given the word of wisdom through the Spirit, to another the word of knowledge through the same Spirit, to another faith by the same Spirit, to another gifts of healings by the same Spirit, to another the working of miracles, to another prophecy, to another discerning of spirits, to another different kinds of tongues, to another the interpretation of tongues."

These nine unique gifts testify and witness to the validity of the gospel of Jesus. Jesus said this enabling power would be a witness to the world. Acts 1:8 (NLT) "But you will receive power when the Holy Spirit comes upon you. And you will be my witnesses, telling people about me everywhere—in Jerusalem, throughout Judea, in Samaria, and to the ends of the earth."

The power of God authenticated Jesus through the Holy Spirit. Acts 2:22 (NLT) "People of Israel, listen! God publicly endorsed Jesus the Nazarene by doing powerful miracles, wonders, and signs through him, as you well know."

The disciples used these gifts when sharing the gospel, and people were persuaded. Acts 4:33 (NKJV) "And with great power the apostles gave witness to the resurrection of the Lord Jesus. And great grace was upon them all."

Jesus told us that supernatural signs would follow those who believe in Him Mark 16:17–18 (NLT).

> "These miraculous signs accompany those who believe: They will cast out demons in my name, and they will speak in new languages. They will be able to handle snakes with safety, and if they drink anything poisonous, it won't hurt them. They will be able to place their hands on the sick, and they will be healed."

THE BODY OF CHRIST

Obtaining spiritual gifts is not like going into a store to get which one you want. The Apostle Paul clarifies this by telling us it is the Holy Spirit who determines who gets what gift. 1 Corinthians 12:11 (NLT) "It is the one and only Spirit who distributes all these gifts. He alone decides which gift each person should have."

Why? Because we, as Christians, are like a human body. As the body has different parts and features, so does the Christian community. Each part of the body has a specific function. The function contributes to the whole body. For example, the arm reaches out and allows the hand to take food and place it in the mouth! So, the body of Christ works the same way.

As a Christian, I'm part of the body of Christ. God positions me in the body as a part, and then the Holy Spirit gives me the ability to function in that role. 1 Corinthians 12:18–19 (NKJV) "But now God has set the members, each one of them, in the body just as He pleased. And if they were all one member, where would the body be? We are all working together to build and strengthen the body of Christ."

DESIRE SPIRITUAL GIFTS

There is much debate in Christian denominations concerning the use, relevance, or even accessibility of these spiritual gifts. Our source is not people's opinions or even their experiences. Our source follows the pattern of Jesus and the disciples according to scripture. We should want to see people find clarity when they lack understanding provided by the gifts of Wisdom and Knowledge. We should want people to move mountains with the gift of Faith. We should want to see people physically healed through gifts of Healing or a miraculous intervention through the gift of Miracles. We should want people to understand things about the future from the gift of Prophecy. We don't want people to be deceived; we need the gift of Discerning Spirits. We don't know how to pray correctly in every circumstance; we need someone to pray in unknown Tongues. If God has something to say to us, we need someone to speak with the gift of Interpretation.

Can anyone have these gifts? Yes! The scripture is clear: these gifts come wrapped in the person of the Holy Spirit, and He is promised to you. Acts 2:39 (NKJV) "For the promise is to you and to your children, and to all who are afar off, as many as the Lord our God will call."

The Holy Spirit, who dwells within us, has these gifts available for us.

What am I saying? You should desire for God to give you one or more of these gifts so that you can help others. 1 Corinthians 12:31 (NLT) "So you should earnestly desire the most helpful gifts…"

IMPARTATION BY TOUCH

The next question is, how do I get these special abilities or experience them? Receiving these spiritual gifts is often called being baptized in the Holy Spirit. When the Holy Spirit came in the book of Acts chapter two, He settled on a group of one hundred twenty believers, and they started speaking in these languages they had never learned. We went into much detail in chapter four about this moment and its significance.

You remember that three thousand people were saved because of this supernatural experience the one hundred twenty people gathered had. Then we mentioned the five thousand who were saved in Acts chapter 3 because of the gift of healing, restoring a man's legs. These 8,000 individuals didn't receive the Holy Spirit the same way the one hundred twenty did. This is where the laying of hands comes in. The one hundred twenty took what they had freely received from God and imparted it to others. Look at what the Apostle Paul says to the church in Rome, Romans 1:11 (NKJV) "For I long to see you, that I may impart to you some spiritual gift, so that you may be established."

When I was a junior in high school, I really pursued Jesus. The church I attended was Victory Tabernacle Assembly of God. The pastor had invited a guest evangelist in for a week of revival services. Brother Noble Gammon was a passionate revival preacher. After the message was given that night, he invited anyone who wanted to experience the baptism of the Holy Spirit forward. I eagerly went to the altar. Standing there in line with a few others, he passed by laying his hands on my head and saying, "Receive the Holy Spirit."

In an instant, I started speaking in unknown tongues. To be honest, it startled me and even scared me initially. I was fully aware that my mouth was speaking these strange syllables. I even tried to stop, but I kept going for about 60 seconds. It was an experience I will never forget. I was baptized in the Holy Spirit.

My experience is not a one-size-fits-all. Your experience may look and feel different from mine, and you may not get the same gift I received. The Apostle Paul explains that everyone is not called and gifted the same; we are a body of diversity. 1 Corinthians 12:29–30 (NLT) "Are we all apostles? Are we all prophets? Are we all teachers? Do we all have the power to do miracles? Do we all have the gift of healing? Do we all have the ability to speak in unknown languages? Do we all have the ability to interpret unknown languages? Of course not!"

Laying on hands is a foundational doctrine in Christianity. It's one of the ways we give what we have to others. We lay hands on people to impart the Holy Spirit. The story in Acts chapter 8 best illustrates how it works. The evangelist Philip is preaching in Samaria. People are being saved and baptized in water. The Apostles Peter and John hear of this revival in Samaria and go down. While people have been saved and were baptized, they have not been baptized in the Holy Spirit. So what did they do? They started laying hands on them, and people were baptized.

> Acts 8:15–17 (NKJV) "Who, when they had come down, prayed for them that they might receive the Holy Spirit. For as yet He had fallen upon none of them. They had only been baptized in the name of the Lord Jesus. Then they laid hands on them, and they received the Holy Spirit."

The apostle Paul comes across some disciples of John the Baptist and asks them if they have received the Holy Spirit. When he discovered they had not, he lays hands on them. All of a sudden, these special abilities start manifesting. Acts 19:6 (NKJV) "And when Paul had laid hands on them, the Holy Spirit came upon them, and they spoke with tongues and prophesied."

The apostle Paul encourages Timothy not to neglect using his spiritual gifts, which were imparted by the Holy Spirit when he had hands laid on him. 1 Timothy 4:14 (NKJV) "Do not neglect the gift that is in you, which was given to you by prophecy with the laying on of the hands of the eldership."

When new ministers were being sent on assignment, they would pray over them by laying hands on them. Acts 6:6–7 (NKJV) "Whom they set before the apostles; and when they had prayed, they laid hands on them. Then the word of God spread, and the number of the disciples multiplied greatly in Jerusalem, and a great many of the priests were obedient to the faith."

They laid hands on people who were in need of physical healing, and they received healing. Acts 28:8 (NKJV) "And it happened that the father of Publius lay sick of a fever and dysentery. Paul went in to him and prayed, and he laid his hands on him and healed him."

The Holy Spirit provides a witness to the world in very convincing ways through you. Laying your hands on someone is a practical way of expressing your faith in Christ. The Holy Spirit that dwells in you will show up in the touch. It's just your hand that does the touching, but it's the Holy Spirit doing the work. Let Him use your hands!

UNORTHODOX

People can feel uncomfortable with this teaching. But this is not about the style of church you attend. You can't have the attitude that we don't do that in my denomination. Baptisms and the laying on of hands were Jesus' ideas. After His water baptism, the Holy Spirit came upon Him (Matthew 3:16), and He started laying hands on people. Luke 4:40 (NKJV) "When the sun was setting, all those who had any that were sick with various diseases brought them to Him; and He laid His hands on every one of them and healed them."

While it can feel odd and uncomfortable, it's the outcome we are after. Let me tell you, Jesus was the most unorthodox of all the New Testament people. One day, He's going to heal a guy who's blind; look what He did. John 9:6 (NKJV) "When He had said these things, He spat on the ground and made clay with the saliva; and He anointed the eyes of the blind man with the clay."

Another time, He's passing a deaf guy, who couldn't speak. Jesus doesn't lightly lay His hand on the guy's shoulders. He goes for the ears and tongue. Mark 7:33 (NKJV) "And He took him aside from the multitude, and put His fingers in his ears, and He spat and touched his tongue."

The blind man was healed, and the deaf man heard and spoke. What wouldn't we do to see that? There may be moments when it doesn't make sense to the mind.

Trust the Holy Spirit. He'll use your hands.

Aren't these the outcomes we're after?

NO GOING BACK TO KANSAS

I am forever grateful for our time at the Baptist Church. I'm also thankful for the unique experiences at that Pentecostal Holiness church. I'm pretty sure neither one of them had it all figured out. I can say that with certainty, and neither do I. There's so much more to learn and do. If we are going to build according to the pattern Jesus taught, we're going to have to risk it occasionally.

Dorothy in The Wizard of Oz only had to click her heels together to return to where she started. I'm sure it was more comfortable and a lot safer to be back in Kansas. But we're after outcomes! If we are to get biblical outcomes, we will have to dig our heels in and refuse to be talked out of it, no matter how unorthodox it may seem.

Over these last three chapters, we've established four critical doctrines of faith that are necessary to ensure we make the final steps! Let's keep walking this out.

CHAPTER TEN

The Resurrection

*

"The entire Bible pivots on one weekend in Jerusalem about two thousand years ago..."
- D.A. Carson

When I went to church as a kid, after presenting his message, the preacher would come to what is called "the invitation." This was the opportunity to invite anyone into the life of faith by saying the "sinners' prayer." It would sound something like this: "With every head bowed and no one looking around, I want to ask you a question: if you were to die tonight, where would you spend eternity? There's no promise of tomorrow. For someone, it could be your last day. If Jesus came right now, where would you spend eternity? If you are here today and you don't want to die lost and go to hell, then slip up your hand and say I want to give my life to Jesus." He would then say, "Everyone that raised your hand, I am going to count to three, and I want you to run down to this altar: One, two, three, run down here now." And there we would go, running from hell.

That preacher was going to do everything he could to get you to accept Jesus Christ, and sometimes, his strategy was to threaten you with eternity. After all, no one wanted to go hell!

Today, you don't hear much of what was called hell, fire, and brimstone preaching. There's not much talk about heaven, either. Unfortunately, the conversation of eternity is not often placed at the forefront when wrestling with the decision to follow Jesus. We certainly are not raising the possibility of "this may be your last chance." Often, the invitation is wrapped around finding freedom from sinful bondage today and for a better life tomorrow, which is a great reason to give your life to Christ. I know that my drug addiction had taken over my life, and I was on the brink of losing it all. I cared nothing about heaven or hell. I felt like I was living in hell already. I needed the hope of a better day, and I found it.

A large proportion of today's preaching is anecdotal to current life circumstances. While I'm not advocating scare tactics to force a decision; I am saying it's incomplete. Life after death is foundational for every follower of Jesus. Furthermore, it must be the end goal in which we live. Why? It raises the seriousness of everything. It puts all of life at stake. It makes every decision eternal. We must understand that we are headed to the best life, the eternal life. If not, we may find ourselves frustrated when Monday doesn't look like the promise you said yes to on Sunday.

The next foundation stone upon which your spiritual life will be built is the resurrection of the dead. Hebrews 6:1–2 (NKJV) "Therefore, leaving the discussion of the elementary principles of Christ, let us go on to perfection, not laying again the foundation of repentance from dead works and of faith toward God, of the doctrine of baptisms, of laying on of hands, of resurrection of the dead, and of eternal judgment."

Repentance, Faith, Baptism, and the Laying on of Hands are what you do in this life. When it comes to the resurrection of the dead and eternal judgment, they are the consequences of what you did. This includes everyone: those who believe in Jesus and those who do not, those who are both persuaded and devoted to God, those who hate Him and want nothing to do with Him and those who did good things in His name, and those who lived a good life without faith—all of us!

CORNERSTONE

In biblical times, there was no concrete to pour into the foundations of the house being built. They used large stones for the foundation and built the structure on top of them. The first stone laid in a foundation was called the cornerstone. It was laid precisely on the corner of the structure, and all the other foundation stones were aligned and leveled with it. Once that foundation was laid, then the house could be built. Jesus is the Cornerstone of our lives. He's where it all starts. The apostles and prophets in scripture align their teaching with the cornerstone, completing the foundation. You and I are the house; we build our lives by standing on this foundation by faith. Ephesians 2:20–21 (NLT) "Together, we are his house, built on the foundation of the apostles and the prophets. And the cornerstone is Christ Jesus himself. We are carefully joined together in him, becoming a holy temple for the Lord."

While Jesus is the Cornerstone of God's work in the earth, the resurrection of Jesus Christ is the cornerstone of the gospel. Without the resurrection, there is no salvation, no reason to repent, no one to confess faith in, nothing to be baptized into, no purpose for the Holy Spirit, and no reason to witness to others. Without the resurrection, there is no promise of eternal life. 1 Corinthians 15:14–15 (NLT) "And if Christ has not been raised, then all our preaching is useless, and your faith is useless. And we apostles would all be lying about God—for we have said that God raised Christ from the grave. But that can't be true if there is no resurrection of the dead."

The good news is that three days after His death, Jesus was resurrected, the grave was empty, and many people witnessed the empty tomb of our risen Savior.

1 Corinthians 15:3–8 (NLT) "I passed on to you what was most important and what had also been passed on to me. Christ died for our sins, just as the Scriptures said. He was buried, and he was raised from the dead on the third day, just as the Scriptures said. He was seen by Peter and then by the Twelve. After that, he was seen by more than 500 of his followers at one time, most of whom are still alive,

though some have died. Then he was seen by James
and later by all the apostles. Last of all, as though I
had been born at the wrong time, I also saw him."

His followers saw Him brutally beaten and crucified on the cross; they saw the empty tomb and touched with their own hands the risen Savior. I heard someone say once that "people have died for a lie they believed to be the truth, but no one dies for a lie they know to be a lie." The apostles were witnesses to His resurrection. They gave their lives to prove it.

Church history has documented the horrendous way in which they gave their life for the truth they knew to be the truth. The early church fathers wrote about how Peter died in Rome by crucifixion during the persecution of Nero in AD 64. They say that during the crucifixion, Peter asked to be crucified upside down, considering himself unworthy to be crucified in the manner of Jesus (Oakes). Can you imagine such conviction? The only way Peter relents to such a horrible death is that he has witnessed with his own eyes the resurrection of Jesus. All the Apostles surrendered their lives in awful ways, testifying to the resurrection. They were convinced because they were witnesses!

Many people have died on crosses throughout history, but none got out of the grave. Many people were resurrected in scripture, but all of them died again. Jesus is the only one who died on the cross, rose out of the grave, and continues to live unto this very day. That makes Him in a class all by Himself. The Apostle John, the last living apostle of Jesus who wrote the book of Revelation, said this in Revelation 1:17–18 (NLT) "When I saw him, I fell at his feet as if I were dead. But he laid his right hand on me and said, "Don't be afraid! I am the First and the Last. I am the living one. I died, but look—I am alive forever and ever! And I hold the keys of death and the grave."

Come on! Jesus is alive forevermore! That is good news for you and me.

The resurrection validated and initiated Christ's claim and promises, which is why the resurrection is the cornerstone of the gospel message. You can build your life on the solid rock of Jesus because He rose from the dead.

GOD'S PROMISE TO YOU

God gave His Son's life to prove His love for us, but the resurrection was how God proved His promise of eternal life to us. John 3:16 (KJV) "For God so loved the world, that he gave his only begotten Son, that whosoever believeth in him should not perish but have everlasting life."

When the followers of Jesus in the Book of Acts launch out into their ministry, establishing the church on the earth, the resurrection is central to their message. Acts 2:32 (NKJV) "This Jesus God has raised up, of which we are all witnesses."

However, their message was not only did Jesus rise from the dead, but those who put their faith in Him would one day be resurrected. Acts 4:2 (NLT) "These leaders were very disturbed that Peter and John were teaching the people that through Jesus there is a resurrection of the dead."

We live our lives of faith because we know we're heading to a better life in eternity—one that will never experience the pain and sorrow of life as we know it. One day, every tear will be wiped away, and death will no longer be a threat. Revelation 21:4 (NLT) "He will wipe every tear from their eyes, and there will be no more death or sorrow or crying or pain. All these things are gone forever."

We access this eternal home through the resurrection.

TWO RESURRECTIONS

Two resurrections will occur in the future: the resurrection of Jesus' followers and those who were not followers. Let me make a clear factual statement: every person will be resurrected and live forever. We'll discuss where eternal living will happen in the next chapter.

The first resurrection will be the followers of Jesus. Revelation 20:5–6 (NLT) "This is the first resurrection. (The rest of the dead did not come back to life until the thousand years had ended.) Blessed and holy are those who share in the first resurrection. For them the second death holds no power, but they will be priests of God and of Christ and will reign with him a thousand years."

When Jesus returns, every person who has died with their faith in Him will be called out of the grave and given transformed bodies. They will have a body like Jesus had when He was resurrected. The Apostle Paul describes what will occur:

> 1 Corinthians 15:52–54 (NLT). "It will happen in a moment, in the blink of an eye, when the last trumpet is blown. For when the trumpet sounds, those who have died will be raised to live forever. And we who are living will also be transformed. For our dying bodies must be transformed into bodies that will never die; our mortal bodies must be transformed into immortal bodies. Then, when our dying bodies have been transformed into bodies that will never die, this Scripture will be fulfilled: "Death is swallowed up in victory."

Just like Jesus came out of the grave, so will everyone who has died with faith in Jesus. The ground will open up, the sea will cough up, the ashes will give up, and the scattered will be gathered together, receiving a new body that can never be corrupted or destroyed again. A new body! I can't wait! We get to trade this one in! I hope to have six-pack abs in the next one.

A side note to Jesus' return and resurrection. There will be people alive upon His return. They, like those dead, will be instantly transformed. Together, we will be gathered from the earth's four corners and meet Jesus in the air. You must read this passage of hope.

> 1 Thessalonians 4:13–17 (NLT) "And now, dear brothers and sisters, we want you to know what will happen to the believers who have died so you will not grieve like people who have no hope. For since we believe that Jesus died and was raised to life again, we also believe that when Jesus returns, God will bring back with him the believers who have died.

> We tell you this directly from the Lord: We who are still living when the Lord returns will not meet him ahead of those who have died. For the Lord himself will come down from heaven with a commanding shout, with the voice of the archangel, and with the trumpet call of God. First, the believers who have died will rise from their graves. Then, together with them, we who are still alive and remain on the earth will be caught up in the clouds to meet the Lord in the air. Then we will be with the Lord forever."

This is what theologians term The Blessed Hope. So whether you have died or are still alive, when Jesus returns, we will all be "caught up" and be with Jesus for all eternity.

THE SECOND RESURRECTION

While those of faith in Jesus are discovering the new world of eternity, there will be another resurrection. Jesus describes it this way- John 5:28-29 (NLT) "Don't be so surprised! Indeed, the time is coming when all the dead in their graves will hear the voice of God's Son, and they will rise again. Those who have done good will rise to experience eternal life, and those who have continued in evil will rise to experience judgment." Jesus said all will be resurrected. Not only be resurrected, but all will live forever.

Right before God sets the eternal city of heaven in place, He will resurrect all those who have "continued in evil," which simply means denying Jesus with their lifestyles and choices. This setting will be at the great white throne described in Revelation 20:11. There will be no escape for anyone. The Apostle John writes in Revelation 20:13 (NLT) "The sea gave up its dead, and death and the grave gave up their dead. And all were judged according to their deeds."

All of humanity who has ever lived that was not part of the first resurrection will be called from the grave, given an eternal body, and stand before God to be judged and sentenced. No prayers or pleading will be answered with grace at this time. No excuse will render God's justice unrighteous. We will share more on this moment in the next chapter.

Every spirit being and every human being will confess that Jesus is Lord, but their confession will merely be an acknowledgment of what they denied or cursed while living. It will not be a saving confession. Philippians 2:10–11 (KJV) "That at the name of Jesus every knee should bow, of things in heaven, and things in earth, and things under the earth; And that every tongue should confess that Jesus Christ is Lord, to the glory of God the Father."

All will be brought into humble submission and recognition of the supremacy of Christ.

Everyone will confess Jesus is Lord. Only those who confess in this life will live with Him forever.

THE CONCLUSION IS COMFORT

Jesus said the day of His return and the resurrection will be preceded by many signs and wonders, including wars, famines, diseases, and natural disasters (Matthew 24). Don't allow life or circumstances around you to discourage you; find comfort in knowing that the best days are coming soon. The Apostle Paul continued in 1 Thessalonians 4:18 (KJV) "Wherefore comfort one another with these words."

The resurrection is to bring comfort that the life of faith that requires sacrifice and discomfort at times is worth it all. It comforts us to know that we will one day be reunited with our loved ones who have gone on before us and the One who died and rose again.

Without the hope of the resurrection, we would be miserable. 1 Corinthians 15:19 (NLT) "And if our hope in Christ is only for this life, we are more to be pitied than anyone in the world." But we have a better life built on some great promises from God.

Maybe you, like me, found Jesus on Sunday just to have a better Monday. Maybe your decision had nothing to do with eternity. That is okay! However, you will still face challenging times of testing and doubt, along with financial and physical challenges. Stay encouraged by reminding yourself of your eternal promises. Live with eternity in mind; you will make the best impact in your time here on earth.

After the Resurrection, there is only one final step.

CHAPTER ELEVEN

Eternal Judgment

*

"Heaven is real, and hell is real, and eternity is but a breath away."
- Billy Graham

When I was growing up, I always had the tendency to be a rule breaker. I pushed back on boundaries and authority constantly. My sophomore, junior, and senior years of high school were the only grades I failed to get paddled. That's right, once upon a time, the teacher could paddle you in school. I've had many. At home, my mom would send us after the "switch." For those who don't know what that is, it is a limb from a tree. She would use that to replace a belt. It would leave marks. I've even celebrated and encouraged others to do things they shouldn't.

My younger brother Shawn decided to steal some padlocks from a local convenience store. Well, as long as he was stealing, he might as well get me one, was my conclusion. So I sent him back to the convenience store to get me a lock. Only this time, he got caught. My mom called my dad, who came to the house with the belt. I remember being perplexed about why I was getting a spanking for my brother's conduct. That was some kind of whipping I got that day. It left marks, too. One mark for sure is I never sent my brother back to do that again. Looking back, I understand precisely why I deserved punishment for encouraging my brother to break the boundaries and not live in them. I was responsible for him. I knew better.

BLACK AND WHITE

As I got older, I continued to experience negative outcomes due to my carelessness regarding boundaries. Even today, my wife and I joke about how she is an extreme rule follower, and I continue to break the rules. She sees everything as black or white, but there is always some gray area for me.

When it comes to Christianity, most of us live in the gray area. We're not good with boundaries, and we very seldom consider outcomes. However, when eternity is considered, there is no gray area. God is very clear.

The final stone to be laid in this foundation of elementary principles is Eternal Judgment. Hebrews 6:1–2 (NKJV) "Therefore, leaving the discussion of the elementary principles of Christ, let us go on to perfection, not laying again the foundation of repentance from dead works and of faith toward God, of the doctrine of baptisms, of laying on of hands, of resurrection of the dead, and of eternal judgment."

In this chapter, we will discuss the severe consequences of the choices we make in this life. The Bible calls it eternal judgment because this ruling stands for all eternity. This is not "time out," so you can think about what you did and resume playing. This is not "get a belt" and then return to activities. This is not "you're grounded for a week," and you can have your phone back. This will not be a temporary punishment or celebration. No, it's final, and it goes on for eternity.

The Lord has set the moral standard and defined the boundaries for us from the beginning. Every time throughout history in scripture, when His people would violate those boundaries, it came with consequences. In Genesis 1, He told Adam and Eve not to eat from the tree of the knowledge of good and evil. They did, and there was consequence. They were driven from the garden, a type of heaven on earth. In Genesis 18, when Sodom and Gomorrah had no righteousness remaining in them, God destroyed the cities with fire.

He gives us direction, boundaries, and protection for our lives. We can choose to live within the boundaries, stay in the garden, and escape the fire.

One thing is for sure: God has given us a clear picture. There is no gray area!

JUDGMENT OF ANGELS

There are three types of Eternal Judgments in Scripture. One is the judgment of Angels. There was a group of Angels who rebelled against God. Jude 6 (NLT) "And I remind you of the angels who did not stay within the limits of authority God gave them but left the place where they belonged. God has kept them securely chained in prisons of darkness, waiting for the great day of judgment."

God gave these angels boundaries to operate within, and they left them. The boundaries were their interactions with humans. These beings sought to destroy mankind. Satan, also called Lucifer, is one of these fallen angels (Luke 10:18). Some are currently held imprisoned until that day of judgment comes. 2 Peter 2:4 (NLT) "For God did not spare even the angels who sinned. He threw them into hell, in gloomy pits of darkness, where they are being held until the day of judgment."

Yet there are some of those angels, like Satan, who are still on the prowl- 1 Peter 5:8 (NLT) "Stay alert! Watch out for your great enemy, the devil. He prowls around like a roaring lion, looking for someone to devour."

As we near the end of the world as we currently know it, these roaming angels and those chained will appear before the Lord and receive judgment. Along with Satan, they will be sentenced to eternal hell for their rebellion. Revelation 20:10 (NLT) "Then the devil, who had deceived them, was thrown into the fiery lake of burning sulfur, joining the beast and the false prophet. There they will be tormented day and night forever and ever."

These angels will be banished to the lake of fire we call hell for all eternity.

JUDGMENT OF SINNERS

The second judgment is for unrepentant sinners—those who rejected Jesus. Back to the great white throne, I spoke about the last chapter. The Bible states in Revelation 20:11–12 (NLT), "And I saw a great white throne and the one sitting on it. The earth and sky fled from his presence, but they found no place to hide. I saw the dead, both great and small, standing before God's throne. And the books were opened, including the Book of Life. And the dead were judged according to what they had done, as recorded in the books."

From the day that you are born, you've been writing your biography in how you think and live. Every detail is being written.

There are only two ways to stand before God: forgiven or unforgiven. If you stand unforgiven, you are responsible for paying the penalty for your sins. In His justice, God will bring the record of your life out into the open. All the secrets you've kept and hidden things you've done, along with all that was known, will be revealed, and you will answer for it. Romans 14:12 (NLT) "Yes, each of us will give a personal account to God."

After giving an account of your life, God will announce His verdict. The penalty for sin is death (Romans 6:23). Those who are unforgiven will be sentenced to a second death by being thrown into a lake of fire. Revelation 20:14–15 (NLT) "Then death and the grave were thrown into the lake of fire. This lake of fire is the second death. And anyone whose name was not found recorded in the Book of Life was thrown into the lake of fire."

All who go to this eternal lake of fire will live eternally in this dead state with consciousness. Jesus, on many occasions, describes the environment as a very dark place with constant crying out from the torment (Matthew 25:30).

There is only one way to avoid paying the penalty for your sins: faith in Jesus. He paid the price if we are willing to believe and follow Him. Some people say, why would God send people to hell? Let me answer this. Everyone born is on a pathway to destruction due to sin. In God's love, He sent His Son to pay the price so we could escape the judgment to come. Our part is to accept it and follow Him.

It's a no-brainer!

HEAVENLY REWARDS

The third eternal judgment will be for those who are forgiven—those whose names are written in the Lamb's Book of Life. Notice there are books, and then there is the Lamb's Book (Revelation 20:15). As previously stated, all of us are writing our autobiography in life. You have a book, and I have a book (Psalms 139:16). The difference for the followers of Jesus is that our sins will be blotted out of our books, and we will not be responsible for paying the penalty of sin. (Psalms 51:9). Jesus paid our price. God will never hold them against us again. He forgets about them.

> Hebrews 10:17 (NKJV) "then He adds, "Their sins
> and their lawless deeds I will remember no more."

When you are committed to putting your faith in Jesus and following Him, your name is written in the Lamb's Book. This book holds the key that grants access to heaven. If you're in the book, you get to go into heaven. If your name is not here, you are cast out. John, describing the heavenly city of Jerusalem, said this in Revelation 21:24–27 (NLT):

> "The nations will walk in its light, and the kings of
> the world will enter the city in all their glory. Its gates
> will never be closed at the end of day because there is
> no night there. And all the nations will bring their
> glory and honor into the city. Nothing evil will be
> allowed to enter, nor anyone who practices shameful
> idolatry and dishonesty—but only those whose
> names are written in the Lamb's Book of Life."

When I said the third judgment is for the followers of Jesus, you are probably saying, "Getting to walk on streets of gold in heaven and see Jesus doesn't look like judgment. Living in a place where there is no more death, destruction, sorrow, and shame in the presence of the Lord is certainly not what I call judgment." And you would be right, well, to some extent. This is part of the reward! Please read Revelation 21 for a deeper description of the heavenly city called New Jerusalem.

MY RESPONSIBILITY

As Christians, our responsibility is greater than simply saying the sinner's prayer and getting our names written in the Lamb's Book. My name in His book means I'm forgiven, and the price for my sin has been paid. However, I'm still responsible for my life of faith.

The Apostle Paul raises the stake of our responsibility as Christians by saying in 2 Corinthians 5:9–10 (NLT) "So whether we are here in this body or away from this body, our goal is to please him. For we must all stand before Christ to be judged. We will each receive whatever we deserve for the good or evil we have done in this earthly body."

Most Christians think it's only a sin issue. It's not. It's a responsibility issue. When Adam and Eve were placed in the Garden of Eden, they were without sin but still had responsibility. Genesis 2:15 (NLT) "The LORD God placed the man in the Garden of Eden to tend and watch over it."

Sure, they had the tree they could not eat from as a boundary, but they also had an assignment. Genesis 1:28 (NLT) "Then God blessed them and said, "Be fruitful and multiply. Fill the earth and govern it. Reign over the fish in the sea, the birds in the sky, and all the animals that scurry along the ground."

These new humans made in God's image and likeness were assigned to reproduce His likeness in all the earth. As Christians now born again in God's image, we bear the responsibility to take this gospel of good news into all the world and make disciples (Matt 28:19-20). What we do with this responsibility will be judged.

There is no better example than in Matthew 25, where Jesus likens the Kingdom of God to a man who journeyed into a far country, which He's speaking of Himself. Before He leaves, He gives His servants talents and abilities; that's us. One servant, He gave five talents; to another servant, He gave two talents; and to the third, He gave one. After a time away, He comes back (we're waiting on His return now). He calls those servants before Him and requires them to give an account of what they have done with the gifts and talents He had bestowed upon them.

One by one, they come before Him, and He rewards them based on their performance and stewardship. He didn't evaluate them equally. He held them accountable for what He had personally assigned to them. This is what Paul is talking about in 2 Corinthians, where he says, "We must all appear before the judgment seat of Christ." This is not the great white throne judgment seat. This judgment seat is likened to those who would judge the Greek games in the old days, like our Olympics. After a runner ran his race, he would come before this judgment seat and receive his rewards. You and I are running in a race (Hebrews 12:1). We have been given great gifts and abilities from God, and one day, you will stand before Him and give an account of what you did with your Christian life.

Here is another way the Apostle Paul describes it:

> 1 Corinthians 3:11–15 (NLT) "For no one can lay any foundation other than the one we already have— Jesus Christ. Anyone who builds on that foundation may use a variety of materials—gold, silver, jewels, wood, hay, or straw. But on the judgment day, fire will reveal what kind of work each builder has done. The fire will show if a person's work has any value. If the work survives, that builder will receive a reward. But if the work is burned up, the builder will suffer great loss. The builder will be saved, but like someone barely escaping through a wall of flames."

Living your life of faith out loud and impacting the world is like gold, silver, and jewels. Living for yourself and showing no concern for the world is building a life out of wood, hay, and straw. When you stand before God, He will test your works and reward you accordingly. Sure, we're going to be saved, and sure, we're going to get access to heaven because our names are written in the Lamb's Book of Life, but there are other rewards that God wants to give us for our sacrifice and service while living on this earth. As we rise to the challenge of being fully devoted followers of Jesus, those rewards are unspeakable.

BRING IT HOME

Some people will say, "As long as I get in, I don't care." Our responsibility extends broader than simply getting in. Our responsibility is to use our key to open the door so that other people can gain access through our life, our example, and our encouragement.

Back to the story of my younger brother stealing those padlocks. I knew there were consequences. I knew there would be a bad outcome if he continued that behavior. Not only did we get a spanking from our father, but he was arrested and taken to jail. I could have prevented that, but I didn't. I am grateful for the discipline my brother and I got that day. He never was arrested for stealing again. The correction reinforced the boundaries. There are boundaries as you walk this life of faith, you will miss it occasionally. God will not give you a pass. He'll show up and correct you. It is never out of His anger or disappointment in you. It will always be to bring out the best in you so the world can see Him.

IN A NUTSHELL

Once the Apostle Paul gave his readers an understanding of this coming judgment seat of Christ, he said this:

> 2 Corinthians 5:11 (NLT) "Because we understand our
> fearful responsibility to the Lord, we work hard to
> persuade others. God knows we are sincere, and I
> hope you know this, too."

The greatest injustice that we will ever give to this world is not to tell them about Jesus' death, burial, resurrection, and eternal judgment. That's the greatest injustice! Leaving people in their sin when I could have been a lifeline, pulling them out and bringing them into eternal life. The best gift that you could ever give someone is the gift of eternal life through the gospel of Jesus Christ. You don't have anything better to give anybody.

You can't help all the poor people on this planet. You can't feed every hungry belly on this planet. You can't pay everybody's electric bill. You can't buy everybody the car they need. But you can give everyone who crosses your path a living example of the gospel of Jesus. You can open the door for them to have a relationship with God that will last for all eternity.

Now that you have the right foundation let's teach it to others. Hebrews 5:12 (NLT) "You have been believers so long now that you ought to be teaching others…"

One of the greatest injustices is to know the truth and tell no one. Take the next step, tell the truth.

SECTION THREE

Picking Up the Pace

Hebrews 6:1 (NLT) "So let us stop going over the basic teachings about Christ again and again. Let us go on instead and become mature in our understanding…"

CHAPTER TWELVE

The Final Step

*

"...when I grew up, I put away childish things."
- The Apostle Paul

No one has played a more significant part in my life of faith than my mother. She rose to the challenge as a single mother raising four kids. We were more than a handful. She did it while standing firm in her faith. It seemed as if our whole life revolved around the local church. She wasn't just a Sunday morning church attender. She was incredibly active throughout the ministry. As I said earlier, we were very poor. She worked as a night auditor for a local hotel, making $3.35 per hour.

Needless to say, we didn't have much of this world's goods at home, yet she would be faithful in giving to the church and helping others in all kinds of ways. Back then, it seemed she preferred those things over our needs. But looking back, she was living out her faith as a mature woman of God.

Over the last eleven chapters, we have led you step by step toward establishing you in the life of faith as a fully devoted follower of Jesus. You have learned that true spiritual maturity is built on the consistent practices of elementary principles. However, as you practice these foundational principles, you will discover there is more. There is always more! We will spend our entire lives growing and moving forward with new discoveries about our Lord and His plans and purpose for us. I call it growing up in Him.

MATURITY

The motive of the writer of Hebrews, captured in the context of Hebrews 5:10- 6:3 that we've been exploring, is to give the reader more insight into God's plan so that they can grow in their maturity. Hebrews 6:1 (NLT) "So let us stop going over the basic teachings about Christ again and again. Let us go on instead and become mature in our understanding…"

So now that we have the basic teaching down and we are prepared to share them, what are other things we need to know and practice to keep moving forward? They are captured in what is NOT mentioned as the "basic teachings."

Time alone doesn't produce experience. In a recent meeting with our staff members, one of them had returned home and visited the ministry where they grew up. Their observations left them heavy-hearted. They said, "It's possible to have 20 years of history with only one year of experience." In short, they were saying that even though the ministry had 20 years of history, they had been doing the same thing over and over again, reliving the same experience.

God wants us always to be growing and moving forward.

KEY NUMBER ONE

I want to give you three keys to growing into a spiritually mature place. They are incredibly important, and if you don't practice them, you will get trapped in the elementary. So, in the direction of "Let us go on instead and become mature in our understanding," Let's go!

The first key is Valuing Community. Even in the Garden of Eden, God said, "It's not good that man is alone" (Genesis 2:18). You cannot do this alone. We are called the body of Christ (1 Corinthians 12:12-27). To function to the fullest capacity, we must do it together. God will place something you need from Him in someone else. You will need to connect with them to gain access. Ephesians 4:16 (NLT) "He makes the whole body fit together perfectly. As each part does its own special work, it helps the other parts grow, so that the whole body is healthy and growing and full of love."

Let me say it like this: there are some things you can pray into your life, and there are other things you can study and learn on your own, but there are many things in God that you will have to have a relationship with someone to gain access. God will wrap a revelation for you in the life and experience of someone else.

The early church in the book of Acts found this key, and they pulled together and lived their life of faith out loud. Acts 2:46 (NLT) "They worshiped together at the Temple each day, met in homes for the Lord's Supper, and shared their meals with great joy and generosity."

The community gatherings were vital for their growth and for expanding God's kingdom. They were living in a very hostile world towards this new way called Christianity; they found strength together.

As our world is more disconnected from God than ever before. We need a deeper connection to Him, and we find it together. The writer of Hebrews raises the value high in Hebrews 10:25 (NLT) "And let us not neglect our meeting together, as some people do, but encourage one another, especially now that the day of his return is drawing near."

Some people say, "I don't need church to be saved." I fully agree! But! There is always a but. I can't live out my life of faith without the church. The church is God's idea (Matthew 16:18). He knew what we needed. You need community if you are going to move forward. The early church met at the Temple, which is like the local church, and they met in homes, which is like a small group. If you are going to grow strong, you must make going to church a huge part of your life. Don't fit the church into your life. Plan your life around being in the church community. Believe me, you need it, your family will benefit, and others will be deeply impacted.

NEW FACES

One of the biggest challenges you will face is making new friends. It won't work out well if your old friends are not walking in your new way, and you keep spending time together. Choosing new friends doesn't make you better than your old ones or mean you're too good for them now. I spent an enormous amount of time with some very good guys when I was coming up. I loved them, we would fight for each other. We were close.

Relationships are built on common interests. We do things that we like together, and the friendship bond grows. However, the common interest was broken when I began to follow Jesus. I still wanted to hang out with my friends and kept trying to keep the relationship alive. What happened was I kept falling back into old habits. This resulted in distancing myself from going to church, which resulted in more turmoil in my life. I was back to where I started, and maybe even worse.

I can take you to the exact time when my relationship with Jesus moved forward the best, and I never returned to my old lifestyle. It all happened when I made a new friend at a church. We started a small group. It was very small, there were only two of us. Every Tuesday, we would hang out and talk about Jesus. Sometimes, we would go to the local nursing home; other times, we would go to the local jail and speak to inmates or stop at someone's house and share our faith as we drove around. This relationship journey provided opportunities to receive from my friend who had been serving Jesus much longer than I and provided opportunities to share my faith with others. I was growing and moving forward.

Do you want to grow? Join or start a small group with people of faith with whom you share interests. Make it a priority to go to church every week. Build your life around your faith journey and surround yourself with people who want to build with you. You will grow!

KEY NUMBER TWO

Jesus said it like this in Matthew 23:11 (NLT) "The greatest among you must be a servant." I add an interpretation to it by saying, "The greatness in you is discovered by serving." When you serve, your greatness gets exposed. We all aspire to do and be great at something in this world. If you're truly going to be great, you must give time to developing your talent. It takes commitment to the hard work.

The second key is Serving. We need to look no further than the life of Jesus to see this walked out. Jesus lived as a servant. He describes Himself this way in Matthew 20:27–28 (NLT) "And whoever wants to be first among you must become your slave. For even the Son of Man came not to be served but to serve others and to give his life as a ransom for many."

The night before He dies, look at what He did. John 13:14–15 (NLT) "And since I, your Lord and Teacher, have washed your feet, you ought to wash each other's feet. I have given you an example to follow. Do as I have done to you."

He washed feet! Talk about famous last words - be a servant and wash someone's feet. The greatness of Jesus shines through His serving of others. His example should become ours.

I realize that my mom's faithfulness through challenging times was often helped by serving others. As she helped others grow, she grew, and it became what I call a divine distraction from her own problems. One way to minimize your challenges is to help others overcome theirs.

Many people struggle to identify what they feel "called" to do. Don't focus on a calling; focus on serving others. I have a phrase I use to describe how we find our way forward- The Ricochet Effect. I use it to explain how God takes where you are serving and uses a situation to open the door and ricochet you into another place. You wouldn't get to the next place without serving at your starting place. For example, you serve in the parking lot of your local church. You're just being a friendly face, helping people find a parking spot and get into the building. You won't see that as a calling in scripture, but it falls under the definition of serving. But here is how it works. One day, you meet someone in the parking lot, you're having a conversation, and they mention an opportunity. It opens a door and ricochets you into another place of serving. Or someone observes you serving in the parking lot, doing it with excellence, getting to see your gift on display, and they have a place within their organization or their ministry, and they invite you to be a part.

The point is to start somewhere, and God will use your actions to ricochet you to where you need to be. Your local church is a great place to start. Join a team and help others have a better experience during church gatherings. Open your home, lead a group, and give others a place to grow. Volunteer for a local outreach to help your community or go on a mission trip. Whatever you do, you must get started by serving.

A word of warning. The spiritual forces working against you understand the power of serving. Once you start, be prepared for the backlash. The backlash will be a situation at home or work or even in the church that tries to discourage your commitment to serve. You'll feel overwhelmed and think the solution is to stop serving until you get it all worked out. Can I say- DON'T DO THAT! Double down! Refuse to let your greatness be hidden by life circumstances. Stay faithful and watch God.

Jesus lived in and served His community. We must follow His example.

KEY NUMBER THREE

At the end of the day, God is after your total devotion. Matthew 22:37–38 (NLT) "Jesus replied, " 'You must love the LORD your God with all your heart, all your soul, and all your mind.' This is the first and greatest commandment."

Think about those three things- heart, soul, and mind. The heart speaks to your spiritual being, the soul is your desires, and the mind is your thought life. God wants you to love Him with ALL the capacity you have. God wants ALL of you!

The third key to maturity is Generosity. Generosity wasn't listed in the elementary principles we spent the previous five chapters discussing from Hebrews 5-6. Why? Because it's not essential? No! Because giving is not elementary, it's sacrificial. If we are not careful, most of our Christian life will be lived consuming. Back to Hebrews 5, when you should be teaching (giving), you must be taught again (consuming).

Most people use the word love to describe something that brings them pleasure. Whether it is ice cream, a sport, or a person. We love everything that pleases us. The true definition of love is sacrifice, not pleasure. God loved us so much that He sacrificed His Son (John 3:16). He sacrificed by GIVING His Son.

Sacrificing our money instead of buying what we WANT is a true sign of spiritual maturing. Jesus said it like this in Matthew 6:21 (NLT) "Wherever your treasure is, there the desires of your heart will also be." What we do with our money speaks to what we value.

Giving is not only about God having your heart; it also empowers God's work to advance. Our slogan is, "Generosity sets the pace of vision." Taking the Gospel to the world requires resources. The more resources you have, the faster you move. When you give, it's like building platforms for the Gospel of Jesus to reach others. God doesn't require us to sacrifice our sons, but we sacrifice our time, talents, and treasures for His Son because of love.

GIVING AND RECEIVING

There is reciprocity in giving. God is not a taker, He's a giver. When we give, God promises to bless us back. Look at Luke 6:38 (NLT) "Give, and you will receive. Your gift will return to you in full—pressed down, shaken together to make room for more, running over, and poured into your lap. The amount you give will determine the amount you get back."

The measure of response is connected to the sacrifice, not the amount.

2 Corinthians 9:6–7 (NLT) "Remember this—a farmer who plants only a few seeds will get a small crop. But the one who plants generously will get a generous crop. You must each decide in your heart how much to give. And don't give reluctantly or in response to

pressure. "For God loves a person who gives cheerfully."

Have an attitude of generosity. Find joy in watching others being impacted by what you give rather than trying to find joy in what you get.

The challenge for you is to commit to giving consistently. Tithing is a scriptural principle of giving that means ten percent. Giving ten percent was a standard God set in scripture, not as a rule but as an expression of devotion (Deuteronomy 14:22-23). Set a standard of giving a tithe of your income and watch what God will do. Look at this promise in Malachi 3:10 (NLT) "Bring all the tithes into the storehouse so there will be enough food in my Temple. If you do," says the LORD of Heaven's Armies, "I will open the windows of heaven for you. I will pour out a blessing so great you won't have enough room to take it in! Try it! Put me to the test!"

God said try me and see what happens.

I watched my mother faithfully write her tithe check. As I said, she made $3.35 per hour, which is $134.00 per week. Yet she would write that check for no less than $13.40. Now, that doesn't seem like a world-changing amount, but it was the sacrifice that God saw. As a result, we never went hungry or were homeless, and our home was blessed with an incredible amount of love.

Learn to steward what God gives you; allow Him to be the owner. Let Him have ALL of you.

THE CONCLUSION

We started this journey with salvation and ended it with keys to grow mature in your walk of faith. But the journey has no ending. We are walking towards eternity. From here to there, let me encourage you: There is no end to deep places of understanding that God wants to take you. There is no end to the impact you can have on eternity. But it all depends on your commitment to stay fully devoted to Jesus. You will have days when God seems a million miles away. You'll have moments when you doubt it all. You will go through a season where you pour out all you have, and nothing seems to work. You'll have times when you completely blow it.

My encouragement is simple: Get up and take the Next Step. Don't stop!

True spiritual maturity comes with the consistent practice of elementary principles. You have them; now grow!

REFERENCES

Holman Bible Publishers. The Holy Bible: NKJV New King James Version. Nashville, Tennessee, Holman Bible Publishers, 2016.

Otis, John. "How 4 Children Lost in the Amazon Jungle for 40 Days Were Able to Stay Alive." NPR, NPR, 16 June 2023, www.npr.org/2023/06/16/1182630213/how-4-children-lost-in-the-amazon-jungle-for-40-days-were-able-to-stay-alive.

Logos Library System. Oak Harbor, Wash., Logos Research Systems, 1996.

Bible. English. New Living Translation. Holy Bible, New Living Translation. Wheaton, Il, Tyndale House Publishers, 1996.

Cleveland Clinic. "Health Information Library | Cleveland Clinic." Cleveland Clinic, 2019, my.clevelandclinic.org/health.

Hoffman, E.A. Are You Washed in the Blood? 1878. Accessed 23 July 2024.

Lewis Edgar Jones. www.hymntime.com, www.hymntime.com/tch/bio/j/o/n/e/s/l/jones_le.htm. Accessed 23 July 2024.

""Houston, We've Had a Problem" Spoken from Space." ABC13 Houston, 13 Apr. 2020, abc13.com/houston-we-have-a-problem-weve-had-remember-when-history/1869513/.

The Holy Bible: King James Version. 1611.

"George Shuba." Wikipedia, 15 July 2024, en.wikipedia.org/wiki/George_Shuba. Accessed 23 July 2024.

Posnanski, Joe. "In Remembrance of "the Boys of Summer" Author Roger Kahn, Who Found Beauty in the Stories of Underdogs." The New York Times, theathletic.com/1592608/2020/02/07/in-remembrance-of-boys-of-summer-author-roger-kahn-who-found-beauty-in-the-stories-of-underdogs/. Accessed 23 July 2024.

Simmons, Brian. The Passion Translation. Passion Translation, 15 June 2015.

"Smith Wigglesworth Quotes." THE JESUS GATHERING, www.thejesusgathering.org/smith-wigglesworth.html#:~:text=I%20don. Accessed 23 July 2024.

beinzee. "A Gift of a Bible." YouTube, 8 July 2010, youtu.be/6md638smQd8?si=uQjN3yWgR3XSjJWg. Accessed 23 July 2024.

Hagin, Kenneth E. Faith Food Devotions. Tulsa, Oklahoma, Faith Library Publications, 1988.

Vidor, King, et al. The Wizard of Oz. Metro-Goldwyn-Mayer (MGM), 1939.

Oakes, John. What Is the Evidence That Peter Was Crucified

Upside down in Rome? – Evidence for Christianity. evidenceforchristianity.org/what-is-the-evidence-that-peter-was-crucified-upside-down-in-rome/.

Made in the USA
Columbia, SC
15 August 2025

3acc6474-dc89-45e0-97e2-34fee2a1f3a4R03